The Point and Figure Method of Anticipating Stock Price Movements

Complete Theory and Practice

by

VICTOR DE VILLIERS

and

OWEN TAYLOR

The Point and Figure Method
of
Anticipating Stock Price Movements
is the
ONLY METHOD BASED ON
Logical and Scientific
MECHANICAL PRINCIPLES

such as

THE LEVER. . .
THE FULCRUM. .
THE CATAPULT. .

These MECHANICAL PRINCIPLES are all involved in Stock Price Movements

PROFITS ARE AVAILABLE FOR THOSE WHO WILL APPLY THEM

Frontispiece 1

SCIENTIFIC MECHANICS
POINT AND FIGURE OF METHOD CHARTS

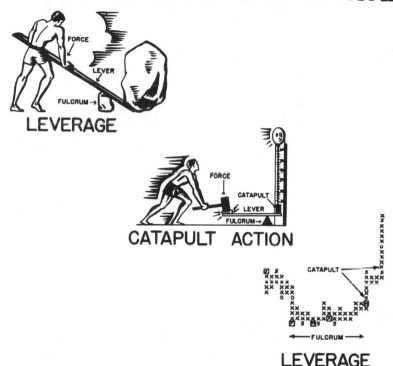

LEVERAGE

CATAPULT ACTION

LEVERAGE

LEVERAGE AND CATAPULT ACTION
CREATE · PROFITS · FOR YOU

This book, along with other books, is available at discounts that make it realistic to provide them as gifts to your customers, clients, and staff. For more information on these long lasting, cost effective premiums, please call us at 800-272-2855 or e-mail us at sales@traderslibrary.com.

ISBN 1-883272-83-1

Printed in the United States of America.

Contents

Authors' Preface xi

I: The Principles of the Point and Figure Method 1

    Logic Is the Basis of This Method 2
    Irrelevant Fluctuations Eliminated 3
    How the Method Got Its Name 3
    Graphs Are Logical and Scientific 4
    Introductory Summary of Important Principles 4
    Needed Accessories Are Few 5
    Plotting a Stock Price Movement 6
    One-Point Charts the Basis of the Method 6
    Accessories and Working Tools 7

II: The Weight of Authority Behind This Method 9

    Refined to Coordinate with Present Day Markets 10
    Mystery and Complications Have Been Clarified 11
    Expensive Financial and Economic Reports Unnecessary 11
    Certain Factors Taken for Granted 12
    Analytical Technic Easy to Master 12
    Losses Limited While Profits Accrue 13
    Method Weighs Forces of Buying and Selling 14

III: Advantages of This Method Over Others 15

    Speed and Ease of Recording Data 15
    The Method Ignores Volume 16
    Price Changes Versus Volume 16
    Supply Versus Demand 17
    Volume Easily Manipulated 17
    Facility of This Method 18

The Utter Simplicity of the Records 18
Manipulation Readily Detected 20
Use All Full-Figure Changes in Making Charts 21
Method Is Superior to Inside Information 22
Isolation Develops Best Results 22
Our Charts Reveal Plans of the Majority 23
How the Move Begins 24
Stock Market Trading Is a Business 25
Inside Information Unnecessary 25
One-Point Charts Show All 26

IV: The Vital Points **27**
Vital Point I – Recording Full-Figure Changes 28
Vital Point II – Only Full-Figure Changes 29
Vital Point III – Suitable Graph Paper 29
Vital Point IV – Use of Horizontal and Vertical Columns 30
Vital Point V – Trend Reversals 30
Vital Point VI – Only One Symbol to a Square 30
Vital Point VII – Move Over Diagonally 32
Vital Point VIII – Skip No Squares 32
Vital Point IX – Formation of Congestion Area 32
Vital Point X – The Full Fulcrum 33
Vital Point XI – First Buying Point 33
Vital Point XII – The Catapult 33
Vital Point XIII – Secondary Buying Point 34
Vital Point XIV – The Semi-Catapult 34
Vital Point XV – Third Buying Point 34
Vital Point XVI – Watch for Distribution 35
Vital Point XVII – Trend Lines 35
Vital Point XVIII – Forecasting the Extent of the Move 35

V: Approved Method of Assembling and
Maintaining Proper Data **37**
The Ticker Tape 38
Source of All Data 38
Daily Full-Figure Fluctuations Available 39
Method Ideal for Those at Distant Points 40
Application of the Data 40

How to Prepare and Collate the Needed Data 41
Proper Graph Paper Helpful. 41
Arrange Charts Orderly 42
How to Select the Issues to Record. 42
Clarifying the Use of the Symbols 43
Moving to Next Vertical Column 44
Use of Symbol "O". 45
One Cardinal Principle 46
Gaps Are Not Recorded 46
How the Gap Occurs 47
Plotting the Gap 48
The One-Point Chart 48
The Three-Point and Five-Point Charts 49
Condensing the One-Point Moves 49
Other Helpful Aids 51
The Method Substitutes for Tape Reading. 51
Trend Outline and Geometrical Charts. 52
The Proper Issues to Chart. 53
Commodity Price Movements 54

VI: The Scientific Fundamentals **57**

The Fulcrum 57
Leverage. 58
Watch for a Fulcrum 58
The Ideal Full Fulcrum. 58
Down Trend a Prerequisite to Fulcrum Formation. 59
Supply Equals Demand 61
Advantage of Figure Charts 61
The Buying Points. 61
The Broad Fulcrum 62
The Recoil Fulcrum. 63
The Catapult 64
The True Catapult. 64
The False Catapult. 64
The Semi-Catapult 67
Use "Stops" to Protect Position 67

VII: The Principles of Charting **71**

    The One-Point Chart 71

        Move to Next Column 72

        Signs of a Fulcrum 73

        Technical Aids 73

    The Three-Point Chart 74

        Determining Three-Point Moves 76

    The Use of Five-Point Charts 77

VIII: Analyzing Technical Position **79**

    The Price Path Characteristics 79

        Patterns of the Leaders Duplicated in the

        Secondary Issues 79

    Solid Formations Give Confidence 80

    Watch for Changes in Activity 80

    Strong and Weak Technical Position 81

        Weak Technical Position 81

    Gauging the Length and Culmination of the Moves 82

    The Count 82

    Coordinating Your Studies 82

IX: Anticipating the Action of U.S. Steel **85**

    The Full Ideal Fulcrum 85

    The Catapult Position 86

    The Semi-Catapult Position 86

    Consolidating the Gains 86

    The Final Mark Up 87

    The End of the Move — A Reverse Fulcrum 88

    The Short Positions 89

    Geometrical Charts 89

    The Trend Outline Charts 89

    The Three-Point Figure Charts 91

    The Five-Point Charts 92

    Summary 92

X: Analyzing a Campaign in Western Union **95**

    Selecting the Fast Moving Issues 95

    The Full Fulcrum Base 96

    The Catapult 97

    The Semi-Catapults 97

    The Short Positions 98

    Summary 99

XI: Judging the Minor Swings **101**

    The Half-Hourly Index of the Dow Jones Industrials 101

    The Half-Point Half-Hourly Log 102

    Half-Point Technic 102

    Scientific Tape Reading 105

    Analyzing the Half-Point Chart 105

    Ignore Rumors and Gossip 106

    Summary 106

XII: Half-Point Technic in Atlas Tack **107**

    Historical Background 107

    Analyzing the Campaign in Atlas Tack 108

    Important Signal During July Break 110

    The First Caution Signal 111

    Boardroom Observations 111

    The Shorts Began to Cover 112

    Point and Figure Analysis 112

XIII: The Main Trend and Major Cycle Culminations **115**

    Critical Culmination Points Easily Detected 115

    The One-Point Chart—The Basis for Analysis 116

    Interpreting an Intricate Major Culmination 116

    The First Temporary Top 116

    Semi-Catapult Point—Unusually Bullish Pattern 117

    Strength Carries Through Objective Level 118

    The Change Over of Technical Action 120

    The Top of the Move Clearly Indicated 121

    Indications of a Major Culmination 122

Bear Trend Technical Action 122
The Investor or Long-Term Trader 123

XIV: Technical Indications at a Turning Point **125**
The Change to an Up Trend 125
The Change to a Down Trend 126

Conclusion **127**

Compendium of Charts — Figures 1 through 30 . . . . **129**

Trading Resource Guide **159**

Authors' Preface

Experiences of the recent bear market which had its termination in July 1932 caused many former investors and traders to turn to the literature of economics and market technic* in order to get a better understanding of the principles underlying stock price movements. Many have come to realize the futility of depending upon tips, rumors and gossip to guide them in their market commitments. Countless others have come to the conclusion that statistics and fundamentals serve only to aid the manipulators, banking sponsors and insiders to unload their stock on the unwary.

All will agree that a correct analysis of the technical position of stocks and the market in general is the only key to consistent profit from speculative and trading commitments.

Until the publication of the original edition of this work, it was the privilege of the few who made fortunes from speculation to have the advantage of this, the most logical and pragmatical of all methods used for the purpose of plotting the price course of stocks and commodities. This Method has been the keystone and bulwark of the plans of America's most successful speculators and commentators, from Charles Henry Dow, the father of the art of anticipating stock price movements, down to and including those who have profited most during 1929 and subsequently.

We offer you the principles of this tried and proven Method because we feel that a broad dissemination of this information will do much to prevent the excesses of bull market peaks and also help avoid the unreasonable

---

* Technic is the spelling the author used in the original text. Today the more common spelling is technique(s).

deflation of values, as well as the vicious cycles of forced selling and the resultant suffering of depression lows which so surely must follow.

We desire to express our appreciation to Mr. J. Martiney of the publisher's technical staff for the many helpful suggestions given and his care in the preparation of the charts used in this work.

We gratefully acknowledge our indebtedness to Charles Henry Dow, William Peter Hamilton, James R. Keene and others whose works and achievements have been an inspiration and a guide.

Victor de Villiers
Owen Taylor
New York City
January 1934

I

The Principles of the Point and Figure Method

Fifteen years before the turn of the last century, Charles H. Dow, student, scientist and philosopher, a brilliant economist and a well-respected financial writer, began to observe and study the phenomena of Stock Price Movements. He was the founder of the *Wall Street Journal*. His writings, though not prolific, are the beginnings of all price movement comment, his observations the foundation underlying all technical methods, and his studies and graphic records the seeds from which the Point and Figure Method grew.

The work of Dow was ably carried on by his protege and successor, William Peter Hamilton, who edited the *Wall Street Journal* until his death in 1929. The writings of Hamilton form the principal source from which Dow's Theory of Stock Price Movements has become available for study.

At or around the beginning of the present century, when the expansion era was in full swing, a group of speculators recognized in Dow's research[1] a clear illustration of price movements portrayed through the use of figures which showed a repetition of pattern as it unfolded its tracings on Dow's graphic records. The patterns thus formed were oft-times repeated, and established a precedent and guide to future price

---

1 See pages 36 and 153 *The Stock Market Barometer* by W. P. Hamilton

movements. Here, then, was the beginning of a truly scientific and logical method of anticipating stock price movements.

Fifty years of background, millions of dollars of profits taken out of the stock market, and thousands of hours of study and development, are historical events which commend this time-tried Method to you.

In explaining the basic principles of the Point and Figure Method, we will show that the full point and full figure fluctuations in variable equities, be they commodities or stocks, are the vital statistics which hold the key to technical position and the future price path.

Professionals and others who have been successful in their judgment and anticipation of market action, have reached their conclusions by aid of recorded data of one kind or another. In practically every field of endeavor, whether it be in the arts or sciences, in the industrial world, or in the stock and commodity markets, full and detailed records of past and current essential data must be kept. It is of little consequence whether these records are maintained as tabulated figures or by means of logs or charts, which are merely graphic representations and plottings of those essential records.

Charts of stock price movements are vital. There is an ancient Chinese axiom dating from the Confucian era which states, "A picture is better than a thousand words." It is self-evident that a picture conveys a clearer and more detailed message than a mass of words or columns of tabulated figures. Since instant comparison and maximum condensation are vital to the art of anticipating stock price movements, we endorse the practice of keeping and maintaining up-to-date charts. Graphic representations of the fluctuations of stock prices are vitally important to a critical analysis of technical position and are the keystone of the Point and Figure Method.

Logic Is the Basis of This Method

Few will dispute the fact that the old-fashioned custom of relying solely upon published statistics of sales and earnings for market commitments, must now be relegated to the past. All will agree that by the time these statistics become available for public consumption, others, principally the insiders, the sponsors and the manipulators, have already profited amply therefrom and are ready to unload their commitments as the news becomes public property. We must, therefore, find a method which will show us when the insiders are buying and also indicate when they are commencing to sell. Given the ability to recognize their acts on our charts, it follows logically that we will be able to buy when the insiders buy and sell out when they sell.

The patterns portrayed on our charts and application of the principles of the Point and Figure Method will show us when buying is overcoming selling and vice versa. If you are ready to agree that the present movement of stock prices, as recorded on the ticker tape, is the best and surest indication of the probable direction of the future price trend, then this Method can be used to show the way.

It should be needless for us to state that some intensive study and a thorough understanding of the principles are necessary before you can hope to capitalize on that knowledge. Once a solid foundation is laid, your judgment will develop in a logical manner, and you will quickly begin to recognize many profitable opportunities. You will be more certain of yourself, and the courage of your convictions will materially increase your capital.

Irrelevant Fluctuations Eliminated

The market fluctuates in countless fractional transactions which, in the final analysis, have little or no influence on future price paths. One of the basic principles of the Point and Figure Method is to eliminate the irrelevant and regard only the important movements upon which our deductions are based. Only full-point changes are considered, and fractional variations are totally disregarded.

How the Method Got Its Name

The Point and Figure Method derives its name from the fact that we record by FIGURES all full POINT changes. This plan or system of plotting

3

and recording the movements of the market in general, and of selected individual stocks, is a basic principle of this particular Method. In this one characteristic, it is totally different from any other plan, method or system of anticipating stock price movements.

Graphs Are Logical and Scientific

A casual glance at the illustrations in this work will show a new kind of chart which, in contrast to all others, has a scientific basis to recommend its use. The Point and Figure graphic records are made up of a series of symbols composed of X's, fives and zeros. The special design of graph paper, which we suggest for use with this Method, shows the relationship of these symbols to each other and to the past and probable future price movement. Familiarize yourself with the form and style of these important aids, namely, the charts upon which we rely for our conclusions. Point and Figure charts condense the price fluctuations in such a manner that you will soon learn to recognize accumulation, mark-up, and distribution and thus be able to make your commitments more profitable.

Introductory Summary of Important Principles

The Method will be fully explained in every detail as we proceed. Each step will be carefully developed and clarified before we proceed with the next. All will be illustrated with examples from recent market action, showing the application of the principles. So that you may have a bird's-eye view of the scope of the work, we list a summary of the important principles underlying the Point and Figure Method.

1. The Method develops the ability to recognize the technical position of individual stocks and of the market in general.

2. The Method is consistent and logical, definite and positive, eliminating, as far as possible, guesswork and emotional influences.

3. The data is recorded in such a manner as to create and force the development of true geometrical and symmetrical patterns easily discernible and classified, and which repeat themselves in the progression of the price path.

4. The patterns thus formed create precedents by which subsequent price movements are easily judged.

5. The Method disregards fractions resulting from minor and irrelevant fluctuations. It also ignores volume. The Method is simple and complete in itself.

6. The Method dispenses with news, fundamentals, statistics and the reasons for price movements. It concerns itself primarily with cause and effect.

Needed Accessories Are Few

The data which we record in order to create the basis for the application of this Method is, primarily, all one-point changes of the price movement as it fluctuates. This principle is the same whether we apply it to stock price movements, market indices, or commodities. As a matter of fact, the Point and Figure Method of anticipating price movements may be applied to any form of equity for which a free and open market exists, and in which there are price fluctuations.

When full-point variations of the price movement are known, they are recorded by figures. Our records are unlike the conventional vertical line or bar charts in that they are created through the use of symbols. The symbol "x" is used to record the digits 1, 2, 3, 4, 6, 7, 8, and 9. The figure "5" is used to indicate figures ending with digit five. The symbol "0" is used to indicate figures in multiples of tens. At this point, it would be well for you to examine the illustrations used in this book in order that you may have a better understanding of this elementary principle used in making our charts.

The full figure one-point changes are recognized by the price fluctuations when they reach each new full one-point change. The change thus noted is recorded, whether it be the next higher or the next lower figure, and the change must be recorded each and every time it shows on the tape. At this point, let us emphasize the fact that herein lies the vast superiority of this Method over all others. When we record all full figure changes, we are better able to detect accumulation, distribution and the characteristics peculiar to the particular stock or commodity under observation. Note, here, that we disregard all movements of seven-eighths points or less, when fluctuations are in eighths. In cases where fluctuations are in tenths or dollars, we must determine whether we will plot the full one-dollar changes or whether the changes in tenths would better serve our purpose.

Plotting a Stock Price Movement

After we obtain the full figure changes, we proceed to make our graphic record from that data. We require for that purpose, graph or charting paper ruled for quick and easy use. Ideal paper for this purpose is "Ideal Charting Sheet Number 5001." This paper is ruled with vertical and horizontal columns, arranged with shadowed symbols "0" and "5," and with the horizontal columns for these important digits accentuated.

The vertical columns on our charts are used to limit the plottings of the price movement as long as it continues in one direction without a reversal. As soon as a reversal occurs, and we find the needed square already occupied, we move to the next right-hand vertical column. This vital principle must be fixed firmly in your mind, as it is the only one that may give you difficulty later on when you proceed to make your own charts.

The Point and Figure Method relies on price changes, only, and the graph paper is designed to properly record those changes. The day-to-day time factor and daily volume are ignored. The columns of squares are scientifically designed so as to permit the plotting of true trend-lines and to force the development of true geometrical and symmetrical patterns which facilitate accurate comparisons and dependable diagnosis.

In the case of a stock selling at $20 per share, we would record the zero in the square on the 20 line. The next record would be made when the stock sells at flat price 21, or at flat price 19. Should it go down to $19\frac{1}{8}$, or up to $20\frac{7}{8}$, no change would be made.

One-Point Charts the Basis of the Method

When a series of full figure one-point changes of a price movement have been recorded, they create a scientific basis from which to draw conclusions. Because of the fact that similar causes usually create similar effects, our conclusions have a dependable basis not available through the use of any other method.

In addition to the one-point charts, one may easily prepare from them either three- or five-point charts or both. These are helpful for gauging the technical position of any and all issues, volatile or otherwise, and for revealing the broader intermediate moves of stocks and the market.

Accessories and Working Tools

In addition to graph paper, one needs a record of the actual full figure changes garnered from the most accurate source, the ticker tape.[2]

When using this especially designed paper and the daily service which is available, it is a relatively simple matter to keep current the needed changes on one-hundred stocks and the important popular averages or indices, in about thirty minutes each day. Form this habit, as it will afford you an opportunity to analyze the patterns as they unfold themselves on your charts and thus take advantage of the implications which develop, first in one issue and then in another. The little effort expended in keeping these charts up to date will soon pay you handsomely, for you will be training yourself in stock market technic in a way not afforded by any other method.

---

2. Full Figure Daily Data published by Stock Market Publications. New York, N.Y.

II

The Weight of Authority
Behind This Method

The Point and Figure Method has grown from a crude beginning which started more than fifty years ago. Charles H. Dow, the founder of the art of anticipating stock price movements, created much which led to the development of the technic of this Method. Dow, in his research, was interested primarily in recognizing the main, broad, long-term trend which results from the movement of major capital into or out of common stock equities. This main trend was rightly termed the "Capital Movement Trend" by Mr. Edwin L. Ayres in his book *Key to Stock Price Movements*.[3] The secondary corrections to the main trend, though of interest to Dow, were not the goal of his efforts. He considered the secondary movements highly misleading and concluded that the shorter day-to-day swings were unimportant.

However, we must bear in mind that since Dow's work was completed, the stock market and America's financial structures have undergone revolutionary changes. Common stock equities of American corporations have attracted a world-wide speculative following, unprecedented in the history of finance and of speculation.

In Dow's era, a move of 20 to 30 points in the Industrial or Rail Index consummated in a period of a few years was considered a complete bull

---

3 *Key to Stock Price Movements—Logic of Stock Market Trends*. Stock Market Publications, New York, N.Y

cycle. Under present day conditions, we note, on occasion, moves of 10 to 20 points in either or both indexes completed in a few weeks. Three-, nine- or sixteen-million share days, such as were recently witnessed, were undreamed of at the time when ten or a dozen stocks were the active trading mediums, and volume was limited to a few hundred-thousand shares a day. One can, therefore, understand why Dow passed lightly over the minor and secondary movements and sought only to ascertain the main trend. These minor and secondary movements have now become all important. Their study, analysis and the understanding of how to use them form the basis of the most successful method of stock price anticipation.

It has been intimated that this Method was first successfully used by James R. Keene during the merger of the United States Steel Corporation in 1901. Mr. Keene was employed by the sponsors of the Steel Corporation to distribute to the public the original stock of the corporation, which its real founder, Andrew Carnegie, refused to take in payment for his equity and profits resulting from the merger.

Mr. Keene, originally a Western mining promoter, was a skilled tape reader, a shrewd observer and a successful market operator. His ability has never been surpassed and rarely, if ever, equaled. It has been stated by his close associates that the Point and Figure Method was known to and used by him during all of his successful campaigns.

Refined to Coordinate with Present Day Markets

Like all knowledge, the Method has developed with the passing of years and has been refined, improved and coordinated with the ever-changing conditions of stock market action. The scientific basis of the fundamental principles underlying the Method alone accounts for its survival while most other methods have been relegated to the past. You may confidently depend upon the Point and Figure Method knowing, first, that it rests upon a sound scientific basis and, secondly, that it is vastly superior to any other plan for anticipating stock price movements. In the past as well as at present, it has been and is relied upon by many of Wall Street's most successful interests.

The data which should be kept will be described in utmost detail. Bear in mind that there is a great weight of authority behind this data, and we ask of you to respect its implications. We have found by the trial and error method those refinements needed to fit the basic principles to present day markets. It was ascertained that a careful checking and rechecking of the conclusions arrived at by means of this Method is of vital importance and cannot be overemphasized.

Mystery and Complications Have Been Clarified

The Point and Figure Method, as here presented, is devoid of mystery and complications and has proven itself of incalculable aid to your authors. We begin by reducing the vast accumulation of transactions comprising market action to the important and relevant moves, which are plotted on charts. From these graphs showing the present market action, we are able to judge the probable future direction and extent of a stock's movement.

The Point and Figure Method permits stock market trading to be considered a serious business with a scientific, substantial and definite background, based upon actual facts rather than guesswork.

Like all other businesses, it demands the making and preserving of certain simple and vital records. It demands that you study those records carefully and permit your judgment to be based upon solid facts. None will deny the old copy book maxim "practice makes perfect." The Point and Figure Method actually compels practice and extensive study which soon becomes a habit as well as a fascinating hobby.

Expensive Financial and Economic Reports Unnecessary

This Method dispenses entirely with the expense and labor involved in the purchase and maintenance of bulky reports, statistics, balance sheets, earnings statements and other cumbersome paraphernalia hitherto associated with trading and investing. The substitution of the simple records required by this Method is, in itself, an important consideration and a welcome relief.

Certain Factors Taken for Granted

The following facts are taken for granted by the Point and Figure Method:

- That the correct valuation of a stock, at any given time, is the price paid for it at the time of the consummated sale. This is because the forces underlying the law of supply and demand and the consensus of opinion of the buyers and sellers have determined the value at the time the sale is made.

- That the last published price of a stock reflects all that is known by the general public at the time when established, as a result of a sale and purchase which consummates a transaction.

- That the insiders, who are presumed to know more about any particular stock than the public, cannot completely conceal their future intentions with regard thereto.

- That the plans of the insiders will be revealed in due time by the technical action of the stock itself.

The Point and Figure Method is not a system for "beating the stock market." It is the result of the rationalization of logical principles successfully used by important market interests.

Analytical Technic Easy to Master

Assuming that the student will keep the required records, there remains only the need of an understanding of the technic of reading and interpreting them. In the pages to follow, we illustrate for you in detail and with clarity the technic of interpreting the patterns which develop on your Point and Figure charts. While proficiency may not come at first, yet, in a short time, through study, practice and observation, the habit of correct thinking in terms of the Point and Figure Method will become apparent, and the resulting sound judgment will soon replace uncertainty and confusion.

It is confidently expected that, as a result of this study, observation and practice, the reader will learn to properly appraise the price movements, analyze the technical condition, and deduce therefrom plausible conclusions, the correctness of which will soon exceed the errors you are apt to make. With proficiency attained, your market operations cannot help but result in profit.

Losses Limited While Profits Accrue

Success in trading and investing, whether by method or by chance, comes not as a result of being perfect, but in consequence of completing a sufficient number of successful transactions netting substantial profits to offset the few errors which may show limited losses.

In order to limit losses and to check possible errors, we employ the simple technical aid known as "stop orders." It is unnecessary for us to go into detail here, as the theory and application of stop orders are fully described in many other works.[4]

In no other enterprise or business is it possible to protect profits or check losses with the same ease and facility as is possible in the stock or commodity markets, through the simple expedient of stop orders. We strongly endorse the use of stop orders except where "averaging" or "pyramiding" is resorted to. Many admonitions have been given against averaging and pyramiding, yet this Method not only tolerates, but, at times, presents ideal points at which both may be resorted to, for the reason that each commitment is independent and is made on its own merits. This will be fully explained in a later chapter.

A pyramid is created when the profits accrued on a position are used to buy additional commitments. This practice usually develops into an inverted pyramid when it is resorted to in connection with credit—borrowed funds—used to finance a margin account. An inverted pyramid is exceedingly dangerous because the load gets top-heavy, as the human weakness to make huge and quick profits invites an overextended commitment, which, as a general rule, is wiped out on the first technical reaction.

---

4 *Stop Orders—How to Use Them for Profit* by Owen Taylor.

13

We average a position by buying additional quantities of stock as it sells lower in the price range. This Method indicates ideal points at which to make additional commitments for the purpose of averaging ones cost.

Method Weighs Forces of Buying and Selling

The Point and Figure Method actually measures the forces of supply and demand, and records the support and resistances at all points. It permits of a wide range of visualization through its lucid, graphic records which allows quick and ready comparison of one stock with others and with the market in general, as reflected by a good index and, most important of all, with its previous technical action. These records, if properly compiled from reliable sources, will indicate the true trend of the market and of stocks, and will point out the best trading and investment opportunities.

The Method indicates when and what to buy. It also cautions when to get out, first, through clear signals to act, then, through definite indications for the logical placement of stop orders. It teaches you to adopt a professional approach to your market transactions. Professionals may be considered as the insiders, pools, independent operators, stock sponsors, bankers and others usually referred to as "they" by many market commentators.

III

Advantages of This
Method Over Others

There are certain definite and inherent advantages of the Point and
Figure Method not possessed by any other method. These advantages are: (a) the elimination of non-essentials, (b) the ease of
condensation and (c) the speed by which results may be achieved. These
superior qualities are again stressed in order to point out that the simplicity of this Method does not curtail its accuracy and dependability. A simple
machine with a few well-constructed parts will operate far more efficiently
than a complicated mechanism with ponderous accessories. So it is with
the Point and Figure Method.

Speed and Ease of Recording Data

The Method provides, amongst other things, clarity and simplicity in the
keeping of its graphic records. This results in the creation of logical and
clean-cut patterns on the graphs and higher speed in the plotting of the
necessary data. It will enable you to maintain the records of more stocks,
and be a source of checking and correlating all of the facts, with a view
of arriving at a correct interpretation of market activity and profiting
therefrom.

The Method Ignores Volume

The Point and Figure Method entirely dispenses with the recording of the volume of sales. Many have felt this to be a distinct deficiency under the belief that volume is a dominant factor. We are unwilling to concede that volume is the vital influence which, in the final analysis, governs the price movement. It is conceded, however, that volume is an influence when used as an aid in other methods. In our opinion, the Point and Figure Method has proven itself so much more reliable, that we are satisfied from our research and experience to conclude that *the number of price changes and the manner in which they combine themselves have a more scientific foundation than the influence of volume in the anticipation of price movements.*

Price Changes Versus Volume

Let us analyze the effect of the influence of volume as against the effect of price change only. What is the aim of all methods which seek to anticipate stock price movements? Do we seek to know how many shares are exchanged? Or, do we desire to determine whether stocks are passing from weak holders into strong hands and vice versa? All will agree that it is the answer to the latter question which will permit us to profit most from our knowledge. Taking for granted the known fact, namely, that each transaction printed on the tape is at the same time a purchase by one and a sale by another, it is of little consequence to know the exact number of these transactions. What we desire to ascertain is where in the price scale they occur and their relationship to each other.

Let us approach the problem in a logical manner by taking note of the definitely known elements, in order to determine whether price changes or volume has most influence.

In a speculative market, where the laws of supply and demand are operative, we must have fluctuations in prices. These fluctuations are due mostly to differences of opinion which cause what is technically known as the bid and asked spread. Experience has taught us that *a great number of fluctuations in a congestion area usually indicates either accumulation or distribution.* When stock is offered for sale at the market, we must take the nearest bid price; and when one is anxious to purchase a stock and offers to take it at the market, he must pay the nearest asked price. The price changes of a stock, as it moves from one price to another, are caused by the difference of opinions of those who are buying and selling. These fluctuations have proven themselves more informative for our purpose than has volume.

Supply Versus Demand

Furthermore, let us consider the effect of supply and demand on any product or commodity, be it stock, equities or horseshoes. When demand is greater than supply, prices move upward. Should supply be greater than demand, then prices are forced downward. When demand has absorbed all the supply at any given price, it will begin to absorb the supply available at the next higher price at which offerings are available. As the demand increases, prices correspondingly increase. Prices recede as a result of absence of demand or an oversupply.

These factors show that price, as such, holds the key to supply volume as well as to demand volume. These fluctuations or price changes, when plotted by means of the principles outlined for you in this book, will more accurately indicate the technical condition, the relationship of supply to demand, than any other known method which can be used for the purpose.

Volume Easily Manipulated

Volume, as well as price fluctuation, can be artificially manipulated. Manipulations of volume at any given price level are deceptive and cannot reveal the difference between true and artificial demand. As contrasted with that principle, consider how easy it is to detect artificial support resorted to for the purpose of distribution when many changes in the price of a stock show that it cannot absorb the supply at the upper registered level, or that demand is insufficient to reach to the next level of supply. This principle becomes more clearly apparent as you compare these conditions in one particular stock with the market and other stocks. Volume indications have a tendency to vary greatly with the changes in the floating supply of stocks as well as changes due to the open short interest in the market. We, therefore, conclude that price changes of themselves, with their relationship to each other and to the market and other stocks for comparison, are vastly superior than is volume, used with any other combination. Herein, then, lies the vital and vast superiority of the use of price changes and the Point and Figure Method.

Facility of This Method

This Method permits and facilitates the easy recording of the essential data, and a simple and logical method of analysis. The direction of the trend, the extent of the move and a reasonable approximation of the culmination thereof, are all easily determinable. Through the aid of the one-, three- and five-point charts, one may be reasonably certain of the shorter immediate swings and the more profitable intermediate trend moves, as well as the main broad swings of the bull and bear market cycles—the Capital Movement Trend.

We can visualize at a glance, through the aids afforded by this Method, namely, the one-, three- and five-point charts, the broad zones of accumulation and distribution in the main swings, as well as the closer areas of supply and demand of the narrower and more speculative intermediate trend moves. Our data shows, at a glance, the moves by important areas, by months, by days, by the all important dividend periods, by seasonal influences and by main business cycle influences. It also shows the results of speculative influences, as well as the effects of long-range investment buying and selling.

The Utter Simplicity of the Records

Remove now from the rear of your binder* Chart Figure 1 (see page 19). Examine this illustration of a hypothetical move from a start and low of

---

* Note from the Publisher: For the convenience of the reader, the charts are inserted after the author refers to them and captions have been added. Please note the original edition was published in binder form and the charts appeared at the end of the text. In keeping with the spirit of the original edition, we have also added the charts at the end of this edition as they would have appeared in the original.

FIGURE 1   One-Point Chart

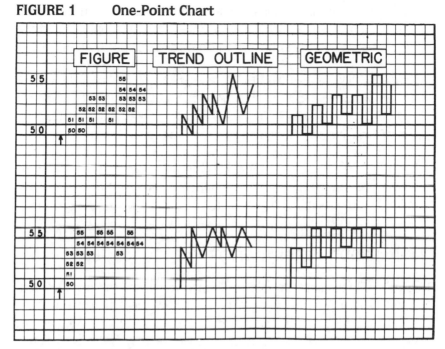

In this one-point chart, we are given two possible price paths—each connoting a different technical condition. The upper half is bearish and the lower half is bullish. Both price paths are illustrated using the three separate and distinct methods by which data may be recorded: figure (left), trend outline (center), and geometric (right).

50, to a high of 55, and a close at 54. Here we illustrate a one-day move which by other methods would not permit of technical analysis, yet by the Point and Figure Method, we are given two possible price paths, each of which would connote a different technical condition.

Note the upper half of the illustration, which we diagnose as bearish. Study carefully the three separate and distinct methods by which data may be recorded when using this Method. The first plan is recording **by figures**. Trace the move, 50, 51, 50, 51, 52, 51, 52, 53, 52, 53, 52, 51, 52, 53, 54, 55, 54, 53, 52, 53, to 54, the close. The pattern just to the right of the figure chart is called a **trend outline chart** and illustrated the same move. On the extreme right you may observe the **geometrical chart** of the same move. Note now that all of this action may be recorded

19

by one day's market fluctuations in a fairly active issue in normal markets. This illustration is bearish because it indicates stock in supply around the 52, and 53, levels with a temporary push through to 55, near the close.

Now regard the lower half of our illustration Figure 1 (see page 19). Trace the move, 50, 51, 52, 53, 52, 53, 54, 55, 54, 53, 54, 55, 54, 55, 54, 53, 54, 55, 54. This move is diagnosed as bullish because it indicates scarcity of offerings below 55, and its ability to hold the advance above 53.

The analysis above is made on the actual movement of the issue as shown. If the immediate previous action was plotted and available for comparison, our diagnosis might change.

Manipulation Readily Detected

Records of fluctuations, upon careful analysis, reveal the manipulation. You have seen in the foregoing paragraph how the action which takes place during any market day is broken up into its important fluctuations, namely, its component parts, in order that we may be able to detect what the manipulators, pool operators, and insiders may be doing with the issue. No method as yet devised will show manipulation as clearly and as surely as a diagram made according to the principles of the Point and Figure Method.

Stock sponsors and operators vary their plans of campaign. Some prefer to depress a stock and make it look very weak, even though it is their aim to mark it up to substantially higher prices. Others, whose tactics are bolder and more open, do not hesitate to bid up the price of a stock very rapidly, taking all blocks offered on the way up, and thus creating a spectacular move. The latter method is daring but very effective, because spectacular moves attract wide public appeal through the aid of board-room traders and others who watch tape action, as well as comments in the newspapers which usually follow spectacular moves as they develop on the tape.

When operators resort to such spectacular manipulation, lively tape action excites gossip in boardrooms and thus attracts a great following for the issue. No matter what procedure is selected by the insiders in any stock, our Point and Figure charts will reveal the areas in which they are accumulating stock and will, with equal accuracy, show zones of distribution.

Use All Full-Figure Changes in Making Charts

Build up your Point and Figure data carefully, using for your purpose either the transactions recorded directly from the tape or the full-figure daily changes supplied by the publishers of this book. When you plot all of the full-figure fluctuations, you have a true representation of what is taking place in the issue. While Point and Figure charts may be compiled from the financial page quotations of your local newspaper, records thus compiled are not nearly as dependable for forecasting purposes as are those with *all* of the full-figure fluctuations.

The charts built up from authentic data consisting of the actual full-figure changes, will always develop patterns in the progression of a move which soon become easy to recognize and classify. A careful study of past performances recorded in the same manner will reveal to the student several important factors which have vital forecasting significance—in that they show the proper points at which to make commitments.

These patterns are created as a result of better buying than selling when the move is in the upward direction, and likewise, when the move is down, they reflect the reverse—better selling than buying. Since a similar cause is always followed by a like effect, these patterns, as they develop, are generally followed by the same type of subsequent action. As we cannot build a house without some kind of foundation, so a stock cannot advance materially unless accumulation has first taken place. Since accumulation will always register on our charts, it becomes but a matter of careful observation and analysis to be able to recognize a move as it is developing and before it really gets started. In addition, we are able to know the exact point at which the risk may be limited while the profit possibilities are preserved to their fullest possible extent.

These characteristic patterns on our Point and Figure charts always develop, no matter what the condition of the market may be. It is immaterial whether it be a slow day with a half-million shares as the average, or a fast session, with five million shares as the average; our Point and Figure charts will reveal, with accuracy, the technical condition of the price movement as plotted and observed.

Method Is Superior to Inside Information

Since it is the purpose of all market analysis to determine the balance between the forces of supply and demand, we seek a means of accurately measuring those forces. Whether demand be on the part of the well-informed insiders, stock sponsors, manipulators or the consensus of opinion; whether it be one or more of the foregoing groups, or whether it results from sufficient outside public participation, it will bring about the same result on our Point and Figure charts. By means of the use of the Point and Figure Method, anyone who will devote sufficient time to the mastery of its principles can place himself in possession of the knowledge that will put him on an equal footing with the influential forces, whether they be insiders or outsiders. No basis for a movement in any stock can be completed without leaving definite indications in its price path, together with their logical implications as the action of the stock traces its movements clearly on our Point and Figure charts.

Isolation Develops Best Results

As a matter of fact, those who apply the principles of this Method and handle their transactions independently are in a better position than members of a syndicate or a pool operation, for reasons later explained. Prices advance or decline because of the operation of the forces of demand and supply. While it is true that major interests, large-scale operators, syndicates and pools can temporarily accelerate or retard a movement, we must, nevertheless, keep in mind that no human force or group can very long obstruct the real trend of the market as it moves, because of influences of general economic cycles.

In the last analysis, all speculative operations, whether undertaken for trading profits or for long-term investment capital appreciation, must be in harmony with the main trend of the capital-movement cycle, or they will result in grief and loss to those who undertake them. Those who operate with one- to five-hundred share lots of a stock are in vastly better position than are the large groups who must necessarily employ thousands and perhaps hundreds of thousands of shares in their operation. The small operator can reverse his position quickly, while the large-scale operator cannot quickly turn about, by reason of the very size and extent of his commitment and the inability of the market to absorb so vast an amount of stock into the floating supply without breaking the movement wide open and causing a major reversal.

Thus, you see that the use of the principles of this Method is more reliable than inside information. We have actual knowledge of the most potent and vital influence, namely, the actual price changes, which must be considered as the verdict of the market resulting from the consensus of all opinions which influence the issue or commodity in which we are operating.

Adhere to the principle of isolation. Turn a deaf ear to all gossip, rumor, inside tips and other information. Your Point and Figure charts are more reliable than any other source of information available.

Our Charts Reveal Plans of the Majority

Our charts reveal, in a condensed form, all that is known to the insiders and unknown to others, about the movement of a stock up to the very last moment. What more can anyone wish to know?

Authentic and reliable inside information must not, and cannot be disclosed. Disclosure may wreck costly plans. When such information is disclosed, it is no longer inside information, and then it is not worth knowing, for it immediately becomes common property and usually develops to be the most costly type of information in Wall Street. It generally leaves you long of stock while the insiders have sold their stock and are out of the market. Remember, the news and information you get is only what the insiders and sponsors wish you to know, and then only after they have profited therefrom.

How the Move Begins

In recent years, the market has more quickly responded to combined pub-lic sentiment. Millions of investors and speculators comprise that public. On occasions, their demands have taken the market completely out of the hands of the insiders. Their inactivity has, at times, upset many well-laid plans of some of the best banking and financial brains in the country. When these millions begin to act or show tentative signs of activity, the alert major interests—the sponsors, bankers, pool operators and insiders—endeavor to anticipate their demands. The insiders and opera-tors can only anticipate and start the move by quickly completing their positions and temporarily taking stock out of the floating supply. This operation is often completed in secrecy during inactive markets, when all offerings are soon absorbed without indications of demand appearing on the tape. Then follows the demand or the beginning of the demand of the outside public. After this buying has commenced, sponsors continue to accelerate the advance in harmony with the trend, buying and selling on balance, so that the value of their position, completed at the lower level, increases, as prices are forced higher.

As an illustration, a syndicate operation may own, let us say, 10,000 shares of a certain issue at an average price of $10 per share. As the price begins to advance, the manager of the syndicate buys and sells on balance, yet always holds at least the amount originally accumulated, until the market price of the stock is far above the average cost of his posi-tion. At the predetermined higher price level, he begins to sell more than he buys and only buys a sufficient quantity to hold the price of the stock at approximately the level at which he wishes to distribute his inventory, accumulated substantially lower down. **These operations are always apparent from the patterns formed by the price changes and por-trayed on our Point and Figure charts.** When you possess this infor-mation, remember, you, too, may be considered one of the insiders.

Students who take this Method seriously and apply themselves to a better understanding of it are in a more advantageous position than the insiders, since, at the first signs of danger, their smaller positions can be quickly liquidated, enabling them to stand aside while the large-scale interests are struggling to complete their campaign.

Stock Market Trading Is a Business

Again, we wish to emphasize this important fact—stock market trading or investing is a serious business and requires careful study and application. No other business offers similar opportunities for gain as often or as quickly as does the stock market. No other business permits one to limit loss or to insure ultimate success as do your transactions in the market, when you thoroughly understand market technic. Remember, your stock market transactions may be closed out quickly or you may reverse your position or protect it by placing strategic stop-loss orders.

In business, it is the major interests who dominate, and the larger the unit, the more efficient can be its management; yet that is not applicable to the stock market. Here, a very large commitment may prevent quick action when speed is essential.

It is well to remember when you hear of inside information that is unsupported by positive confirmation from your Point and Figure charts that many insiders have, in the past, made serious errors. Testimony before governmental committees has revealed only a few of the grave mistakes made by many well grounded in the fields of finance, economics, and banking. Inside opinion, inside judgment or so-called inside Information, may on occasion be very good, but if your transaction is not properly timed, you may be wiped out, notwithstanding the good intentions of your informant.

Inside Information Unnecessary

It is best, at all times, to rely upon logical judgment, the result of conclusions arrived at through a careful analysis of actual facts. It is far more dependable than guesswork, tips, rumors and so-called inside information. Your full-figure changes, your knowledge of their implications, the direction of the trend and your faith in your own self, is all you need when you employ the principles of the Point and Figure Method.

Inasmuch as market knowledge, by and large, is not an exact science, errors of interpretation cause errors of judgment, and hence faulty conclusions may occur on occasions. The most positive indications may be reversed almost momentarily. Therefore, if in the beginning you err occasionally, do not be discouraged. Profit from your mistakes, note the error carefully and resolve never to commit it again. Bear in mind, as you proceed, that coming events are usually anticipated or discounted by major interests and the insiders. When, in the face of bad news on a particular issue, formations indicative of accumulation develop, despite such adverse news, it is wiser for you to follow the insiders than to pay attention to the news, which may have been deliberately released in order to cause the uninformed to dispose of their stocks at a low level.

One-Point Charts Show All

The one-point figure changes, as they register on your charts, reflect all of the buying and selling. When such price changes have completed the pattern, the picture thus formed is the best sort of inside information, since it may be indicative of an impending up move or down move, as the case may be. When your three-point charts confirm the conclusions reached by a study of your one-point charts, you will then have corroborative proof, and your judgment is thereupon confirmed. Should the implications of your one-point charts be confirmed by the three-point and also by the five-point charts of the same stock, then you may consider your knowledge absolute and definite, and you must act accordingly.

Be ever alert and study at all times. Remember, the patterns which are traced on your charts result from the action of individuals. Your chart discloses the balance of all influences. It tells you what is taking place and when to prepare for the move as well as how to take advantage of that information.

IV

The Vital Points

The one-point price fluctuations are the starting base of this reliable and time tried Method of anticipating stock price movements. For the purpose of clarifying the basic principles, we reiterate and codify these principles so as to avoid any possibility of doubt or question.

The Vital Points underlying the Point and Figure Method are as follows:

I   **Record all full-figure fluctuations** registered on the tape.

II   Plot these changes on suitable graph paper through the use of symbols representing the full-figure changes.

III Make no record of a transaction unless a **flat full-figure** change has actually been registered.

IV   Use horizontal columns for specific price levels and vertical columns for price movements continuing in the same direction.

V   When a reversal of the price movement develops, move over to the first right-hand column and plot the subsequent changes of prices.

VI   A square already occupied by a symbol cannot again be used to accommodate another.

VII A move to the next right-hand vertical column must be in a diagonal direction, either one square higher or one square lower than the last recorded full figure.

VIII No square may be skipped; the pattern traced must be a continuous joining of squares.

IX   Be alert to recognize and observe the formations known as congestion areas.

X   Analyze congestion areas in order to properly take advantage of a developing full fulcrum.

XI   Make commitment near base of a full fulcrum with a stop just below lowest point of support.

XII   Watch for the development of the full catapult point.

XIII   Make commitment at the catapult point with a stop close below.

XIV   Watch for the development of the semi-catapult.

XV   Make commitment at the semi-catapult point with a stop close below.

XVI   After an extended advance, be on the alert for first signs of distribution.

XVII   Learn the technic of the use of trend lines.

XVIII   Study and master the principle of the count to gauge the extent of future moves.

Vital Point I – Recording Full-Figure Changes

We have set forth as Vital Point I the fact that we must record **all full-figure fluctuations** which have registered on the tape. Many persons, after a casual study of the Point and Figure Method, may reach the conclusion that Point and Figure charts prepared from newspaper data, that is the opening, the high, the low and the close which are published daily in financial sections of newspapers, are sufficient from which to gather the full-figure changes necessary to prepare our one-point charts. However, this is not the case. One is not able to obtain **all** of the full-figure changes from newspaper quotations. All full-figure changes are necessary because only by recording **all** of them are we able to develop the proper congestion areas, which, in turn, show full fulcrums and subsequent catapult and semi-catapult formations.

There is little advantage to the study and use of this Method unless you make records of **all** full-figure fluctuations. Furthermore, it is absolutely essential to record all of the full-figure changes if we are to depend upon the count method for the purpose of anticipating the extent and probable culminating point of the next move. The technical terms used herein are more fully explained in subsequent chapters of this work.

While it may be truthfully stated that some of the low-priced stocks do not fluctuate a full point during the day, and, therefore, the needed data could be obtained from the newspaper, it must be emphasized that even though we are interested in a low-priced stock which does not fluctuate actively during a trading day, we must plot the movement of the active stocks in order to get the pulse of the market and thus be able to judge the trend and turning points. Even in low-priced stocks, it is difficult to get an accurate analysis of all full-figure changes unless one has access to the tape so as to know whether the high or low was first established and their exact relationship to the close.

Vital Point II – Only Full-Figure Changes

No transaction is recorded on our charts unless it is a flat full-figure change to the flat full figure above or below the last recorded price. A stock may fluctuate seven-eighths points above its last recorded figure, and seven-eighths points below, giving it a total fluctuating band of one and seven-eighths points, before we enter a new change on our graphic records.

Vital Point III – Suitable Graph Paper

Graphs or charts, whichever you choose to call them, are absolutely essential to this Method. These condensed pictorial representations of the course of the price movement with its oscillations, its advances and declines, are absolutely essential to a scientific study of stock price movements. Charts may be made on any kind of paper which is suitably ruled for the purpose. We especially recommend Ideal Charting Sheets for Point and Figure Charts, because they have been carefully designed in order to facilitate the preparation of the charts and permit instantaneous analysis after the records have been completed.

29

Vital Point IV – Use of Horizontal and Vertical Columns

The recommended graph paper for use with this Method is laid out in columns of squares vertically and horizontally arranged similar to a checker board. The lines dividing the vertical divisions are all of uniform thickness. These vertical columns are used for containing the price movement as they continue in the same direction. The horizontal columns of squares are used to represent specific price levels. The lines dividing the horizontal columns vary in their thickness, for we accentuate the columns for the "5's" and heavily accentuate the columns for the "10's." The plan for accentuating the "5" and "10" squares is very helpful for swift recording and quick analysis. In addition, this especially designed paper has silhouetted figures representing the "0's" and "5's," which facilitate quick placement of these particular price levels on the page.

Vital Point V – Trend Reversals

Vertical columns are used to include the price movements in one direction, up or down, until a reversal develops. When a reversal does develop and we require a symbol to be placed in a square that is already occupied, it is necessary for us to move over to the next immediate adjoining righhand column. After the first figure is recorded in a new column, we may proceed either upward or downward from that point, but not both. We must be especially careful to note that in every case we must have more than one symbol in a vertical column.

Vital Point VI – Only One Symbol to a Square

Since no square can be used twice, it is essential that upon reversal of the trend of the stock price movement we move over to the next right-hand column. Each reversal in trend which calls for an "x" to be placed in a square already occupied requires that we move over to the next right-hand column. In cases where a reversal requires only a one-point change, after which the trend is again established in the previous direction, it is not necessary to move over to the next column, for the change in trend would require a plotting in a square above or below the first one used in the new column. This square, above or below, being empty, we proceed to plot our next symbols. Thus, you will see that in no case can we have only one "x" in a vertical column.

To cite an example, let us analyze the move in XYZ, Figure 2. We start plotting the action of this stock at full-figure 34, and indicate an upward move to full-figure 36. After 36, a reversal to 35 is required, but since the 35 square is already occupied, we move over diagonally (never horizontally) to the next right-hand vertical column. Now the up move is again established and we continue in the same column plotting our symbols above the 5, first figure recorded in the new vertical column group.

A similar situation develops on the reaction from 38, back to 37, from the second column in use to the third column. Another like example

FIGURE 2   XYZ One-Point Chart

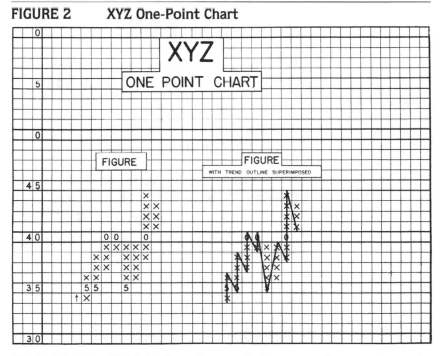

This chart illustrates Vital Point VI — only one symbol to a square. Since no square can be used twice, each time a reversal of the trend of the stock price movement occurs, we must move over to the next right-hand column — diagonally, never horizontally. The trend outline superimposed over the figure chart visually emphasizes this movement.

occurs on the one-point reaction from the first full-figure 40, down to the second 39. Now we come to a difference which develops after the stock rallies from 39, to 40. A sharp subsequent reaction develops and carries back down to 35. Here you see how in one instance a one-point change moves over to the first right-hand column, while another one-point change continues in the same column with subsequent changes again moving over to the next right-hand column.

This is one of the most important principles to be carefully observed in preparing your Point and Figure charts. Study it carefully and know it thoroughly before you proceed with the work. Unless you thoroughly understand the principles of making these important one-point records, you cannot hope to correctly analyze formations which are developed. You cannot hope to arrive at proper and reliable conclusions if you base analysis and deductions on incorrectly prepared data.

Vital Point VII – Move Over Diagonally

This point needs very little further explanation, for it is carefully indicated for you on illustrations throughout the book and fully detailed in our previous paragraph.

Vital Point VIII – Skip No Squares

In the progression of symbols across our graph paper, no square may be skipped. The pattern traced must be a continuous joining of squares of those above, below or adjacent to the diagonal corners. It is only through the proper development of the price path patterns that the important zones of accumulation and distribution will become recognizable. More-over, trend lines cannot be accurately plotted unless the patterns are likewise accurate and symmetrical.

Vital Point IX – Formation of Congestion Area

The most important pattern that will develop on your charts is that which is known as the congestion area. It represents what is technically known as a trading range and shows the struggle between the forces of supply and demand, either at the bottom of the move where accumulation is being completed or at the top of the move where distribution is taking place. At intervening points on the rallies and declines, congestion areas of minor significance form as a result of temporary consolidation. You will soon learn to recognize the importance of the several different types of congestion areas which are formed on your charts.

Vital Point X – The Full Fulcrum

The most important congestion area to form on your charts will be the full fulcrum. A full fulcrum congestion area develops after an extended down move when the forces of demand overcome the forces of supply and a base is formed, followed by two or more attempts to rally. The first indication of strength occurs after accumulation begins at the bottom, when a sharp up move develops and subsequently fails with a recession to the previous support point or to a point slightly above the previous support level. Here, after a little backing and filling, the stock develops technical strength and a new rally carries it higher than the last previous high point, at which point, a full catapult develops.

Vital Point XI – First Buying Point

When you are sure that a full fulcrum is in the process of formation, it is wise to make a commitment as near to the base of the congestion area as is possible, with a stop placed just below the lowest point of support. This is the best place to establish your long position, for here you have the opportunity of gaining the greatest number of points advance with the least possible risk, limited through the employment of a "stop order."

Vital Point XII – The Catapult

The second important place to establish your long position "on stop" is the full catapult point. The law of probability strongly points to the fact that you will quickly see profits after establishing your position at this point. The true full catapult which develops after a full fulcrum has been completed, normally shows from 3 to 6 points profit before a technical correction registers a paper loss on your position. The "stop" used to protect this long position should be placed one point below halfway between the low of the base in the fulcrum and the full catapult point.

Vital Point XIII – Secondary Buying Point

Never fail to take advantage of every full catapult as it develops on your chart. Occasionally you may err and suffer temporary paper loss, but in the vast majority of cases, the full catapult point always develops quick profits for a position established there, especially at the inception of an intermediate or main uptrend following a protracted period of declining prices.

Vital Point XIV – The Semi-Catapult

The semi-catapult is somewhat similar to the full catapult with the exception that it develops during the advance. After a stock moves off the base known as a full fulcrum and an extended move is in progress, it hesitates and forms temporary congestion areas on the way up. These small congestion areas, usually resulting from minor technical reactions during the advance, create semi-catapult positions as soon as the strength in the stock registers a new high price over the high previously established before the technical reaction.

Vital Point XV – Third Buying Point

Make a long commitment at the semi-catapult point each time it develops. Protect this position with a "stop order" placed just below the lowest point established on the technical reaction preceding the semi-catapult figure. You may occasionally lose one or more of these positions and suffer the loss of a point or two between the semi-catapult price and your stop order. However, your losses will be limited while your chances for profits are far in excess of the probability of loss. Profits will accrue to this position in more than six out of ten times established, which profits should be far in excess of losses, especially if the "stop order" suggestion is followed.

Vital Point XVI – Watch for Distribution

After an extended advance, be on the alert for the first signs of distribution. A trading range or congestion area which is built up after a sharp advance in price will be the point for you to watch for first signs of distribution. Use a "stop order" if you are in doubt, or sell on strength soon after you have recognized the beginning of distribution. Technical aids for determining signs of distribution will be found in Book 2 entitled *Advanced Theory and Practice of the Point and Figure Method.* *

Vital Point XVII – Trend Lines

Trend lines are helpful technical aids to use in conjunction with your Point and Figure chart. The technic of the use of trend lines is fully described in the advanced book prepared for students who have already mastered the principles outlined in this book.

Vital Point XVIII – Forecasting the Extent of the Move

The "count" principle of gauging the extent of future movements can be applied by those who have thoroughly mastered the elementary technic of the Point and Figure Method. Through the use of certain well-established scientific principles, your Point and Figure charts will show the probable culmination point of the next move. The system of the "count" is highly technical in its character and fully described in the *Advanced Theory* of this Method.

---

* Note from the Publisher: This book is no longer available.

V

Approved Method of Assembling and Maintaining Proper Data

We have made clear to you the fact that this time-tried Method depends for its accuracy upon a radical and entirely different principle. Price changes, that is the fluctuations in the price of a stock, are more important as the basis upon which to judge its technical condition than are either volume or price range. Price range is the zone between the high and the low which the stock registers each day.

A carefully compiled transcription of these price changes will point the way to more consistent and greater profits, with less guesswork and more confidence in your market commitments.

Before we begin to make the chart, it is most important that we obtain the exact price changes in the order in which they occur, and that we be certain of the source of our data. It is vital and most important to the proper application of this Method that we obtain *all* of the price changes and plot them *all*. The most vital signals given by this Method are those occurring in the trading ranges, the congestion areas, either at the termination of moves at bottoms and tops, or in the consolidation areas, during the advance or decline.

A trading range is the zone in which a stock backs and fills, i.e. fluctuates above the level of support where sufficient buying is encountered to absorb all offerings and the resistance level above where the demand is unable to absorb the supply. A trading range is sometimes called a "line movement" especially when it is used to describe this action on the part of a market index. In the latter case it shows the base, that level at which sufficient capital is available and desirous of being exchanged for stock, and the resistance level above where the holders of stock desire to exchange their equities for cash.

It, therefore, becomes evident and is of vital importance that all fluctuations be obtained from reliable sources and that they be carefully recorded in the order in which they occur.

The Ticker Tape

Many years ago, Stock Exchange authorities recognized the importance of creating and preserving actual records of all transactions as they occur on the floor of the Stock Exchange. It was then that the ticker tape, as we know it today, was conceived. In the beginning, the records were crude, but as the market broadened in the number of corporate issues traded and this country grew in wealth and importance, the ticker became more highly developed, so that now it is capable of high speed, and the price fluctuations are printed almost as quickly as they occur. It is only on rare occasions that the new, high-speed ticker lags, a few minutes at most, behind the actual transactions.

Source of All Data

The ticker tape is the official Stock Exchange record of all transactions, and it automatically becomes the source of all data for this or any other method of anticipating stock price movements. Whether you are guided by vertical line bar charts, by moving averages, by statistical information, business conditions or by the actual technical condition of the stock itself, the source of all information as to the price, the range, the daily closing, daily, weekly, monthly or yearly, high and low prices, or actual price fluctuations, the ticker tape is the original source of all information. All errors which occur in the recording of the transactions effected on the floor of the

New York Stock Exchange are quickly corrected on the tape, sometimes within a minute or two after the error occurs. The ticker tape, therefore, is considered the very best source from which to get the price fluctuations so vitally necessary to the use of the Point and Figure Method.

Daily Full-Figure Fluctuations Available

It is not necessary for you to be in your broker's office in order to procure all of the full-figure fluctuations. The publishers of this book provide that service, and it is published daily. In order to insure the accuracy of the information, they have a trained and skilled staff of men who read closely all transactions on the ticker tape.

Each morning, the previous day's changes are carefully checked against data supplied by the Stock Exchange blue sheet and the three most reliable daily financial publications. Errors, if any occur, are carefully noted by the service on the succeeding day in a special errata column.

In the less volatile issues it is possible to approximate the full-figure changes from the stock market quotations as published in your daily newspaper. Price fluctuations compiled from newspaper openings, highs, lows and closes, are not nearly as dependable as the information garnered directly from the tape. In one case, you are assured of all full-figure fluctuations, while in the other, a great number of full-point changes may be missed. This is vital and important because as you proceed with your work, you will soon realize that complete campaigns of accumulation and distribution can be effectuated in one, two or three market days. As a general rule, Point and Figure charts compiled from newspaper quotations will rarely show a complete fulcrum, catapult or semi-catapult formation. These formations will develop when you plot **all** of the full-figure fluctuations.

Just as a house cannot be built unless a foundation or base is first laid, so a stock cannot rally to any degree, as a general rule, without first creating a congestion area or base from which to advance. Therefore, you must realize that in order to have fullest advantage from your knowledge of the Point and Figure Method it is absolutely essential that you record all of the full-figure fluctuations.

Method Ideal for Those at Distant Points

For students and observers at distant points, this Method offers a splendid opportunity for observation and study. Even though your *Full Figure Daily Data* may be three or four days late in arriving, your charts will always tell the story in ample time for you to have fullest advantage of moves as they develop.

If you are a great distance from New York City and cannot get the accurate full-figure changes, we suggest the following procedure. Obtain from your brokerage office, customers man or daily newspaper, your tentative full-figure fluctuations, and enter them on your charts by making pencil dots in the squares representing the temporary and estimated changes. A day or two later when you receive your accurate full-figure changes, carry forward your chart in ink. Thus, you will have the opportunity of being right up to the minute on the few stocks in which you may have a commitment, and when authentic figures arrive, you are assured of having the correct changes for inking in your graphic records for future reference and study.

Application of the Data

After you are certain that you are obtaining all of the authentic full-figure fluctuations, it is well for you to form the habit of recording the changes each day. It is best to maintain charts of at least fifty, and if possible, one-hundred active stocks, as well as of the following averages, namely, the Dow Jones Industrials, the Dow Jones Rails, the Dow Jones Utilities and the New York Herald Tribune Index of 100 Stocks.

A one-half point chart compiled from figures representing the half-hourly running line of the Dow Jones Industrial Averages is also very informative of the nearby minor swings. Elsewhere in the book, we supply full detailed explanations of this half-point, half-hourly running line index.

For the sake of emphasis and clarity and in order to give the student a proper start, we describe, hereunder, the different types of charts which may be built up from the basic data, namely the one-point figure changes.

How to Prepare and Collate the Needed Data

It is of vital importance that you keep all the needed data in a uniform, neat and compact arrangement. The authors have devoted serious thought to this problem and the publishers have designed a series of special charting papers which are ideal for the purpose.

Proper Graph Paper Helpful

We recommend and use, exclusively, "Ideal" charting sheets #5001, printed on white paper, for our one-point charts; #5003, printed on buff paper, for our three-point charts; and #5005, printed on blue-tinted paper for our five-point charts. No. 5001.5, our half-point paper, is especially recommended for fractional Point and Figure charts. Nos. 5001, 5003, and 5005, are printed on good quality rag stock, 8½ x 11, and are perforated for the conventional three-ring binder. These sheets are convenient to inspect, easy to remove and ideal for the purpose of study and comparison. The ruling, especially designed, presents a simple arrangement for the digit, ciphers and full-figure fives.

The sheet is so laid out that it may be read at a glance with the minimum probability of error. The price level is quickly realized, so that in going through your binders of charts, your attention can be concentrated on a study of technical conditions rather than on irrelevant details.

All of the charts reproduced in this book were drafted on these special "Ideal" charting sheets. The sheets are printed in a special color of ink which permits you to make your charts in pencil or in ink. When using pencil, the special color of the background graph lines permits the pattern to stand out in contrast to that background, even though you use a hard #3 pencil, which permits the plotting to be made without smudging, as is sometimes the case when a softer pencil is used.

As you progress with your work, you will soon be able to keep a graphic record of the movements of 100 stocks and five averages within the one-half hour period.

Arrange Charts Orderly

The charts kept in your loose-leaf binder should be segregated into one-, three-, and five-point groups. Since the sheets are printed on different colored paper stock, one may easily differentiate them and quickly select the desired chart. The arrangements within the binder may be altered in accordance with your personal preference. We have found it more convenient to group the charts in alphabetical order according to the name of the stock. In this way, comparisons and daily changes are made quickly and easily.

One need not feel that the pressure of other affairs will prevent one from mastering this Method. Primary records, the one- and three-point charts, can be kept and maintained by any clerk or stenographer. Any intelligent assistant, after a little preliminary study of the principles of this Method, can keep all the needed data and pass on the finished work for study and analysis.

How to Select the Issues to Record

In selecting your group of stocks, it is well to include a minimum of fifty of the most actively traded issues. Whether or not you intend to trade in any or all of these stocks is of no consequence. In addition to the individual issues which it is important for you to keep, it is wise to record the movements of at least three or four of the important popular averages. We suggest the Dow Jones 30 Industrials, the Dow Jones 20 Rails, the Dow Jones 20 Utilities and the New York Herald Tribune Averages. The Dow Jones Averages are shown and quoted wherever American stocks are traded in. The Herald Tribune Average is a weighed index of 100 stocks and a better, truer, and more ideal cross section of the market as a whole. It is less volatile and more dependable due to the fact that it is not easily manipulated.

In addition to the four indexes suggested above, your authors keep and observe a one-half point chart of the Dow Jones 30 Industrials, calculated on a half-hourly interval. The running line half-point half-hourly index is a very helpful aid in determining the short swing trends and their terminations.

While at first glance it may appear that the necessary data hereinbefore outlined will cause an insurmountable amount of work, nevertheless, we want to call your attention to the important fact that the greatest losses in the stock market were occasioned by hasty judgment, want of incentive and lack of knowledge of actual market action.

Investment and trading is a serious matter. If you desire to succeed and take profits from the stock market, you must expect to work and study. The work is interesting, the necessary materials inexpensive, and the compensation far in excess of the value of the effort and time consumed.

If you want to have the greatest benefit from your knowledge of this time-tried Method, we urge you, once more, to keep and maintain the one-point moves in 100 stocks and five averages and the three-point moves for the same group. Five-point charts, which were mentioned before, are not absolutely essential. They are helpful and can be used for the important indices in order to aid in judging the main trend, and as condensation charts for the more volatile issues.

Clarifying the Use of the Symbols

Recording these price movements, as we have already explained, is done through the use of three simple symbols, "x," "5," and "0." The symbol "x," stands for any full figure which does not include a five or a cipher. Therefore, the symbol "x" may stand for the digits one to four, six to nine, eleven to fourteen, sixteen to nineteen, and so forth and so on. The symbol "5" represents all the multiples of five, such as five, fifteen, twenty-five, thirty-five, etc. Note here, that the figure "5" is used only where the figure ends in five and not when it ends in zero. The symbol "0" is used to represent all multiples of ten in the progression of the price movement, 10, 20, 30, 40, 50, 60, 70, etc.

Examine, now, one or more of the charts included in this book in order to get a better and clearer understanding of the use of these symbols. Charts show in clear and simple manner how to use the "x," the "5," and the "0," in their proper places in the price progression and the pattern formation which it creates.

Examine Figure 2 on page 45, headed "**XYZ One-Point Chart**." Note how we have illustrated the use of all three of the symbols. The first and lowest "x" represents the full figure 34. The first figure, "5," immediately above the first "x" represents the full figure 35 and indicates a progression in an upward direction from 34, to 35, as the stock moves upward. The "x" above the first single figure "5" stands for 36. This shows a move of two points from full figure 34, to full figure 36, or a move to 36⅞, which would be the fullest extent of an upward move represented by an "x' in the 36 square. The second full figure "5," indicated in the next right-hand column, again represents the price progression and a reversal of the former trend.

Moving to Next Vertical Column

Note, here, one of the most important principles in plotting the price movements by the Point and Figure Method. When the trend direction of a stock changes and the required square is already occupied by a symbol, it is necessary to move over to the next adjacent right-hand column. This is very important and one of the principal stumbling blocks which may give you trouble if you do not thoroughly understand it. The chart of "XYZ" at this point indicates a move in a downward direction, from the previous 36 full figure or 36 and a fraction, to the full figure 35 or 34 and fractions above the flat full figure 34.

After plotting the symbol in the 35 square, the trend again changes, and the price movement progresses in an upward direction. The next full figure required is a 36. Since the 36 square is open, we may plot this by recording our "x" just above the "35" most recently recorded. The move then continues in an upward direction registering 37 and 38, before a reversal takes place. Thereafter, we are required to indicate a downward move to 37 or fractionally lower, and since the 37 square in the column is already occupied, we are required to move over to the first right-hand column. Again the trend changes. Now we require a 38, indication, and the symbol "x" is placed in the square just above the 37 most recently recorded.

FIGURE 2   XYZ One-Point Chart

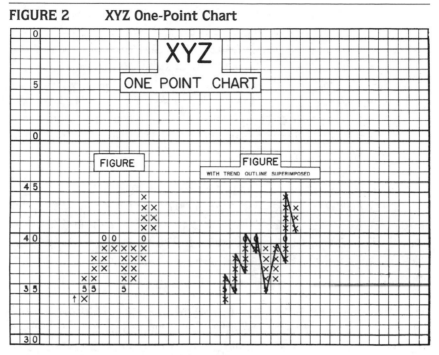

This chart is shown again to illustrate the recording of price movement through the use of the three symbols—"x," "5" and "0." It also shows the symbols in their proper places in the price progression and the pattern formation which it creates.

Use of Symbol "0"

The move continues upward, 39, and full figure 40, is registered. Here we have the first opportunity of using the symbol zero. "0," then, is placed in the square above the 39, on the 40 horizontal line. Thereafter, a down move to full figure 39, is recorded and we find it necessary to move over to the next right-hand column, because the 39 square is already occupied. The stock then rallies to 40, and we plot the 40 above the 39 already recorded. A sharp down move follows, and the stock registers full figure 35, before a change in trend takes place. This requires symbols to be placed in the 39, 38, 37, 36 and 35 squares. Since the 39 square is already occupied, we move over one vertical column to the right and indicate the down move to full figure 35. The stock then rallies to 39, requiring symbols in the 36, 37, 38, and 39 squares in the next adjacent right-hand column. Now a one-point reversal is recorded, requiring us to move over to the next adjacent vertical right-hand column where we plot an "x" in the 38 square. The stock then rallies sharply, making full figure 44, and we proceed with our recording, placing an "x" in the 39, "0" in the 40 square, "x" in 41, 42, 43 and 44 squares. Now a reversal takes place, and the stock sells off making the full figure 41. Again we are required to move over to the next right-hand column in order that we may record our "x" in the square for 44, and we carry to 43, 42, and 41, terminating the move as indicated.

In order to make it clear for you, we have designated the direction of the move by showing a black line superimposed over our symbols on this illustration. Note that we have used the symbol "x" to indicate the prices 34, 36, 37, 38, 39, 41, 42, 43, and 44. The symbol "5" indicates the price 35, and the symbol "0" indicates the price 40, in recording the full-figure changes.

When we commence to plot the movement of a stock with the full figure 34, no change is made until either full figure 35 or full figure 33 is registered on the tape. Thus, should the stock go down from 34 to 33^1/8, no change on our records would be made. Similarly, a move upward to 34^7/8 would be disregarded. You see, therefore, that a stock may fluctuate 1^7/8 points without requiring any change on our Point and Figure data.

One Cardinal Principle

Fractional fluctuations are disregarded unless a new flat full figure is completed. We urge you to trace carefully, again, the move in XYZ by one-point fluctuations as illustrated in Figure 2 (see page 45). Note the fact that fractional fluctuations are completely disregarded. A move which fails to record a new flat full figure is considered of no importance and, therefore, not taken cognizance of.

Gaps Are Not Recorded

Since vertical line bar charts have come into wider vogue, several technicians have laid down certain principles based upon the phenomena known as gaps. Gaps on a bar chart are created as a result of a thin market and occur (1) when the high of a day is lower than the low of the preceding day, and (2) when the low of a day is higher than the high of the succeeding day. Thus, you see, one gap is created by strength, which leaves an opening between the low of the new day and the high of the previous day, and the other by weakness, which leaves a gap between the low of the preceding day and the high point made after the weakness developed.

In vertical line technic, commentators have noted that gaps created by a thin or unusual market are, as a rule and in the majority of instances, closed over sooner or later by subsequent market action. The principle of gaps and their subsequent closings is not to be relied upon in all instances. While it is customary for gaps to close shortly after they are left by market action, it is not a fixed rule, and cannot be thoroughly relied upon. Gaps exist in many issues, both above and below present market action. In rare cases, some take years before subsequent action will close the gap.

The Point and Figure Method completely disregards the gap phenomenon and its theory. Since we are interested in price fluctuations and the recorded trail of the price path, the mere fact that no transaction takes place at any particular point in that path is of little consequence and is not taken into consideration.

How the Gap Occurs

Let us illustrate and show you an actual example of how the Point and Figure Method provides for gaps in the price track of a price movement. Let us assume, for instance, in XYZ, that full figure 38, recorded at the bottom of the fifth rally when the stock moves down from full figure 39 to full figure 38, represents the closing at a particular day, and that overnight some bullish news is released unexpectedly and a sudden demand is created for the stock of the XYZ company. A news item such as "XYZ dividend rate raised from $2 to $4" might create such a situation.

Let us suppose that some trader wishes to buy one-thousand shares quickly, believing that subsequent market action will show good profit for a new position established at this point. He places an order with his broker to buy 1000 shares of XYZ, "at the market." The quotation on XYZ, is: "38½ bid, offered at 40."

The block of shares offered at 40 is only 200, and, therefore, the broker must take 200 at 40, 100 at 40¼, 100 at 40¾, 300 at 41, 100 at 41⅛ and 200 at 41¾. This transaction on the tape would appear as follows:

XYZ   2S40 - 40¼ - 40¾ - 3S41 - 41⅛ - 2S41¾

With the previous close having been registered at 38, these transactions shown on the tape would require the following changes in our graph:

Plotting the Gap

Following the 38 in the vertical column and above, an "x," would be plotted in 39, even though no transaction appeared between the previous 38 and the opening 40. The next symbol recorded would be the zero in the 40 square, and then the "x" in the 41 square, representing transactions up to and including the 200 shares sold at 41¾.

Subsequent action of XYZ for the rest of the day included a continuation of the strength up to 44⅞, followed by a reaction to 41.0 where the stock closed. That action on the tape would be illustrated by a continuation of plotting "x's" in the vertical column up to and including the "x" representing the figure 44, and then the reversal of the trend showing the "x" in 43 moving over to the next right-hand column, then 42, and finally 41, where the stock closed.

Thus, you see, in order to develop the proper technic for creating reliable patterns on our Point and Figure charts, we disregard the theory of gaps since it has no influence on our conclusions.

The One-Point Chart

Since all conclusions and subsequent records are compiled from your one-point charts, it is the best policy to keep them with greatest care. One-point charts should be made in the simplest manner possible and by means of the "x," "5," and "0," symbols hereinbefore described.

While any square ruled paper may be used for this purpose, it is better to use the specially designed paper which is available for this purpose and which will permit the accurate plotting of trend lines and the quick recognition of the 5 and 10 levels, as well as the full fulcrum, the catapult and semi-catapult as they develop.

In order to get a better and clearer conception of market action, it is advisable also to compile a substantial quota of charts and keep them up to date, since a comparison of the patterns formed on the individual charts will enable you better to judge the important trends and the vital turning points. No matter what your plans may be, whether you trade for the shorter swings or invest for the longer pull, you will require these one-point charts. No reliable analysis of technical condition can be made without them.

It is from the one-point charts that we are able to recognize zones of accumulation, the beginning of the mark-up, the vital points at which to place long positions, the critical points at which stop orders should be placed, and, finally, indications of distribution.

The Three-Point and Five-Point Charts

In addition to these one-point charts, we will require, as a check on our work, three-point charts of the same stocks and averages which we have plotted by one-point moves. Three-point charts are a resume of the action and are compiled solely from the moves indicated on your one-point records. These three-point charts enable you to keep a clear picture of the intermediate swings of most stocks. They give a true basis for analysis of the more volatile issues.

Condensing the One-Point Moves

Three-point charts eliminate minor technical fluctuations and show the broader congestion areas. In making your three-point chart, you must always remember that your one-point records must show a move of not less than three points in the opposite direction before it is recorded on your three-point condensation chart.

For example: We start with the figure 40. Your one-point chart must show a move to the figure 43, before any record whatsoever is made on your three-point chart. This move from 40, to 43, would be plotted on your three-point chart in the same manner as it is plotted on your one-point chart. From 43, before we could plot a reversal on the three-point chart, your stock must register a reaction to 40, or lower. However, should it react to 42, or 41, no change would be be made on the three-point chart. Now, in minor technical reactions to 42, or 41, followed by a subsequent rally, which would go above the previous 43, the move would be plotted by one-point moves in the same column on your three-point chart as the price advances above 43. Let us say, for example, that the stock rallies to 47, without a full three-point reversal from 43. The added figures on your three-point chart would be 44, 45, 46 and 47. Thus, you see that your three-point chart will show a straight run from 40, to 47, with no other indications recorded. Temporary declines of less than three points are ignored on this chart, and continued subsequent advances above the previous high prices, should they occur, are carried forward by one-point registrations in the same column. Three-point charts are plotted only of trend reversals which are three or more points in extent. In all other respects, your three-point charts are made in the same manner as are your one-point charts.

The five-point charts condense the price changes to moves of five points or more but not less. They are helpful in connection with the indices when prices fluctuate broadly and when they register in the higher price ranges, such as was witnessed in 1929. Five-point charts are also very helpful in that they simplify the interpretation of the wider moving highly volatile stocks. Issues which advance or decline thirty to fifty points in a single intermediate market cycle must be plotted by five-point moves, since these charts give the most dependable and satisfactory presentation of the technical condition of the issue. Five-point charts are also helpful for the determination of the main and long-term trends. They condense the time factor and show long-term accumulation and distribution, thus indicating the trend or movement of capital as it comes into variable equities—common stocks—near the bottom of a bear market, and as it moves out of variable equities into bonds or other forms of wealth, at or near the top of a bull market. Five-point charts are not necessary for all stocks and need only be kept on the highly volatile issues and the market indices.

The technic of preparing five-point charts is exactly the same as that of preparing three-point charts with the exception that it requires a reversal in trend direction of five or more points before that reversal is plotted. Continuations of direction of trend are plotted by one-point moves until a full five-point reversal is recorded on your one-point chart.

Other Helpful Aids

The three types of charts enumerated above may be considered the foundation and scientific keystone upon which this Method is based. In addition, it is sometimes advantageous to make half-point charts of complete half-point movements in low-priced stocks which do not fluctuate sufficiently by full one-point moves to give a satisfactory record on one-point charts. Furthermore, half-point charts are helpful in plotting the Dow Jones Industrial Index on an hourly, as well as on a half-hourly basis.

The Method Substitutes for Tape Reading

The half-point charts are very helpful for many purposes. They permit the exponents of this Method to entirely eliminate from their operations the need for watching the tape. Under present day market conditions, half-point charts of individual stocks, as well as half-hourly changes, of the Dow Jones Industrial Index comprise a better and far more reliable basis for judgment than can be had from tape reading. Half-point and quarter-point charts are more sensitive and give an understandable basis for a detailed record which is vastly superior to the memory of any human being.

A running line of the Dow Jones Industrial Index, compiled on a half-hourly basis, is very helpful as an aid in determining the narrow swings of the market. The running line index will be fully explained elsewhere in this work. In plotting commodities, it is sometimes helpful to compile your charts on the basis of quarter-point moves or half-point moves, as the occasion requires. In some instances, when the commodity prices fluctuate in money values as expressed in units and tens, our primary data charts can be made of each tenth penny fluctuation. Since we ignore fractions when making our one-point primary charts, we would ignore fractions between the full figure and the half figure in making half-point charts. Quarter-point charts would be made by ignoring all one-eighth point moves.

We urge you, when making your Point and Figure charts, to be sure to get all of the fluctuations.

Trend Outline and Geometrical Charts

Students and observers who are beginning to recognize the importance of a sound knowledge of stock market technic will find the trend outline and geometrical charts exceedingly helpful. Though not absolutely essential in the application of this Method, they are easy to read and very helpful. Geometrical charts are especially helpful since they show the trading range congestion areas and manipulation. They are also of great assistance to those who wish to use "stop orders," for the reason that a clear picture of the trading range limitations is always indicated.

Trend outline charts are made by merely joining the tops and bottoms, the extremes of the moves, with a diagonal line. They are illustrated in Figures 2 (see page 45) and 3A (see page 53). These charts differ from vertical line charts and are sometimes used by vertical line technicians as a condensation of the conventional vertical line charts. They enable one to eliminate the time factor and show the important swings of prices—the trend of speculation.

The geometrical chart is made by plotting the extremes of moves with horizontal lines and joining these horizontal lines by vertical lines, thus creating a geometrical pattern. (See Figure 3B on page 53.)

Both geometrical and trend outline charts may be superimposed upon your one-, three- and five-point charts by plotting the trend outline or the geometrical pattern over your symbols either in ink, or in crayon of different color from that which you use for the purpose of recording your basic data.

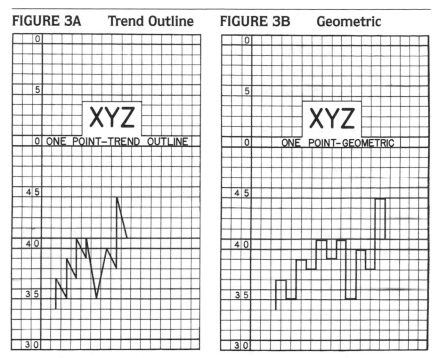

FIGURE 3A   Trend Outline   FIGURE 3B   Geometric

Trend outline and geometric charts are created using vertical, diagonal, and horizontal lines instead of symbols. Trend outlines are made by merely joining the tops and bottoms, the extremes of the moves, with a diagonal line. A geometric chart is made by plotting the extremes of moves with horizontal lines and joining these horizontal lines by vertical lines.

The Proper Issues to Chart

When preparing a set of charts, it is natural and wise to plot the foremost market leaders. From time to time, market leadership will change. Therefore, as one group or one issue loses its popular investment or speculative following, it will be necessary to start charts on the new leaders. The following issues are suggested, at this time, as a good grouping, and, if carefully compiled and analyzed day by day, will guide the student and observer to a proper and prompt recognition of the vital turning points in the market:

    Air Reduction
    Allied Chemical
    American Can

American Smelting
American Sugar Refining
American Telephone
American Tobacco "B"
Atchison
Auburn Automobile
Case Threshing Machine
Celanese
Consolidated Gas
Dome Mines
Du Pont
General Motors
International Harvester
National Biscuit
New York Central
Sears Roebuck
Standard Oil of N.J.
Union Pacific
U. S. Industrial Alcohol
U. S. Steel
Western Union
Woolworth

No two technicians would select or agree upon the same list of leaders; therefore, we leave it to your individual selection to plot and record those issues which suit you best. However, keep a broad group so that the influence of their united action, both from the investment and speculative angles, will guide you in the recognition of important zones of accumulation, the trend of the market, as well as the zones of distribution.

Commodity Price Movements

In a subsequent volume, the authors of this book will show in full detail, application of the Point and Figure Method to the analysis of commodity price movements. The Point and Figure Method has been used successfully as an aid in anticipating the future price movements of wheat, cotton, corn, grain, silver and any other basic commodity dealt in on any Exchange where a free and open market exists and price change fluctuations are carefully and accurately recorded.

As the work applying to commodities is more highly technical and more advanced, this subject cannot be discussed now. Those desiring to use the Point and Figure Method for the purpose of anticipating commodity price movements should and must master thoroughly all of the principles explained in this work as well as in the book *Advanced Theory and Practice of the Point and Figure Method.*

VI

The Scientific Fundamentals

W e have stated that three scientific principles of mechanics known as the **fulcrum, catapult,** and **semi-catapult** are important to this Method and form the keystones upon which it is based.

LEVERAGE

The Fulcrum

In the science of mechanics, the fulcrum is defined as "the support on which a lever turns and the means by which influence is exerted." Leverage is defined as "the mechanical power gained by using a lever." A lever in mechanics is any rigid bar capable of turning about a fixed point and having counteracting forces applied at two other points.

Since the purpose of all observation and study of stock price movements is the determination of the important points from which the rallies and declines have their inception, the pattern known as the fulcrum must be carefully regarded when it develops on your Point and Figure chart.

The fulcrum may develop as a base or as a ceiling near the top of the move where it will form in reverse. It invariably forms at the extremes of an intermediate cycle.

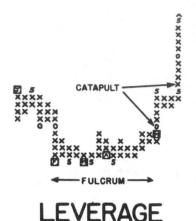

LEVERAGE

Leverage

As in mechanics, where the principle of leverage is operative through the fulcrum point, so on your Point and Figure charts, leverage is created when a congestion area forms a fulcrum after an extended move in the price of a stock. As the course of the price path builds up patterns on your Point and Figure chart, you will begin to notice three types of fulcrums which occur and recur at the vital turning points in the price movement. These patterns repeat themselves very often and with such regularity that you will soon reach the conclusion that no advance or decline of proportions worthwhile anticipating can occur unless the inception of the move arises from one of these three types of fulcrums which we will later describe in detail.

Watch for a Fulcrum

After a base has formed and it develops to be a fulcrum, the leverage there exerted creates a rally of such force and extent that the stock soon reaches the catapult point from which it quickly develops a further sharp upward movement. Therefore, it becomes one of the cardinal principles of this Method to be on the alert and heed carefully the development of a fulcrum formation on your chart. Three types of fulcrums will develop: (a) **the ideal fulcrum**, (b) **the broad fulcrum**, (c) **the recoil fulcrum**.

The Ideal Full Fulcrum

The ideal full fulcrum (see Figure 4 on page 59 and Figure 7 on page 63) always develops at the bottom of secondary culminations and at the top of major swings in new high territory. It may be considered as the head and shoulder formation at the top and the reverse head and shoulder formation at the bottom. It develops as a result of forces, which, when they occur, always create two ideal positions for students of this Method to observe carefully and make long commitments from which quick and substantial profits soon accrue.

FIGURE 4   The Ideal Full Fulcrum

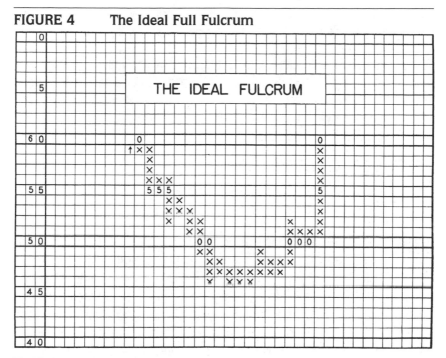

The ideal full fulcrum develops at the point where the center of gravity shows the balancing of the forces of supply and demand. It may be considered as the head and shoulder formation at the top and the reverse head and shoulder formation at the bottom.

Down Trend a Prerequisite to Fulcrum Formation

The ideal full fulcrum develops after a down trend has been halted and the price path builds up a pattern which moves over in the trend channel from the lower trend line to the upper trend line as a result of a series of rallies and declines. This action builds up a congestion area with a flat base. From this series of minor rallies and declines, two to five points in extent, which halt within a limited range developing a flat base, a sharp, quick rally occurs that may result either from short covering or actual buying which creates the short run-up because of the absence of offerings overhead. This sharp advance is then usually followed by a temporary corrective decline which is arrested at a point above the low level established before the first run-up. Subsequent to the second series of rallies and declines, another sharp advance develops which must exceed the high point of the previous rally. The second high point, which is a full figure above the previous rally top, then becomes a ***catapult point***.

Once the stock has developed sufficient strength to hurdle the catapult point, it usually and speedily develops a substantial advance to higher levels, and the reverse occurs when this formation appears near the top of an extended advance.

Supply Equals Demand

The full fulcrum develops at the point where the center of gravity shows the balancing of the forces of supply and demand.

A down trend channel formed prior to the fulcrum point indicates that the supply of stock exceeds the demand. At the fulcrum point, the forces begin to balance. After the first rally where the reaction holds above the previous base level, equilibrium is regained and a new up trend channel is in process of being established. Here, demand begins to overcome supply, and a catapult point eventually develops. At the catapult point, demand has overcome supply, and the advance to substantially higher levels begins.

Advantage of Figure Charts

Complete fulcrums may develop in the market action of one or two days or possibly may take several weeks. On many occasions, Point and Figure charts will show this ideal formation developing while conventional vertical line charts show nothing more than a temporary halt in the down trend. And, in reverse, at the top of a move such conventional vertical line charts would show merely a failure to penetrate the previous top, while your Point and Figure charts would show a complete fulcrum formation in reverse.

The Buying Points

Two important buying points are indicated as the fulcrum develops on your chart. One is in the base, with a stop order placed to limit loss from one to three points below, and the second is at the catapult point with a stop placed below the 50 percent correction level, which must be considered a normal reaction.

The Broad Fulcrum

The broad fulcrum (see Figure 5), which will develop on your charts, requires close observance and careful analysis. It develops as a result of two or more rallies after the base has been formed and will occur after a full catapult has developed but failed to carry through. Broad fulcrums may indicate one of two conditions: either the lack of aggressive sponsorship, i.e. the absence of aggressive buying, or the close balance between the forces of supply and demand. It is well to protect closely a position

FIGURE 5   **The Broad Fulcrum**

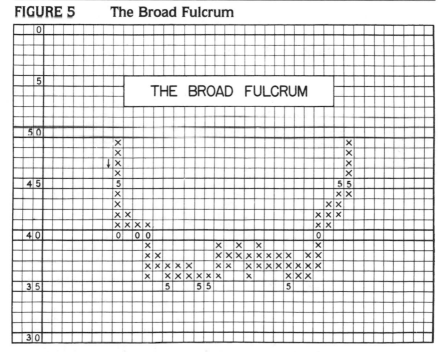

The broad fulcrum develops as a result of two or more rallies after the base has been formed and will occur after a full catapult has developed but failed to carry through.

5 See *Stop Orders* by Owen Taylor.

which has been established in a fulcrum that later develops to be a broad fulcrum. Seek the first opportunity to close out the position by the "stop-order"[5] method after the stock has advanced above your cost price.

The Recoil Fulcrum

The recoil fulcrum (see Figure 6) develops subsequent to a sharp and direct down move after a base forms with ascending bottoms instead of flat bottoms. This type of base usually develops a symmetrical triangle with the vertex occurring just below the catapult point. You will observe that in the recoil fulcrum a catapult position usually occurs a point or two over the vertex of the triangle. Note, then, that this formation develops as a result of a sharp decline followed by sharply descending tops and sharply ascending bottoms.

FIGURE 6   The Recoil Fulcrum

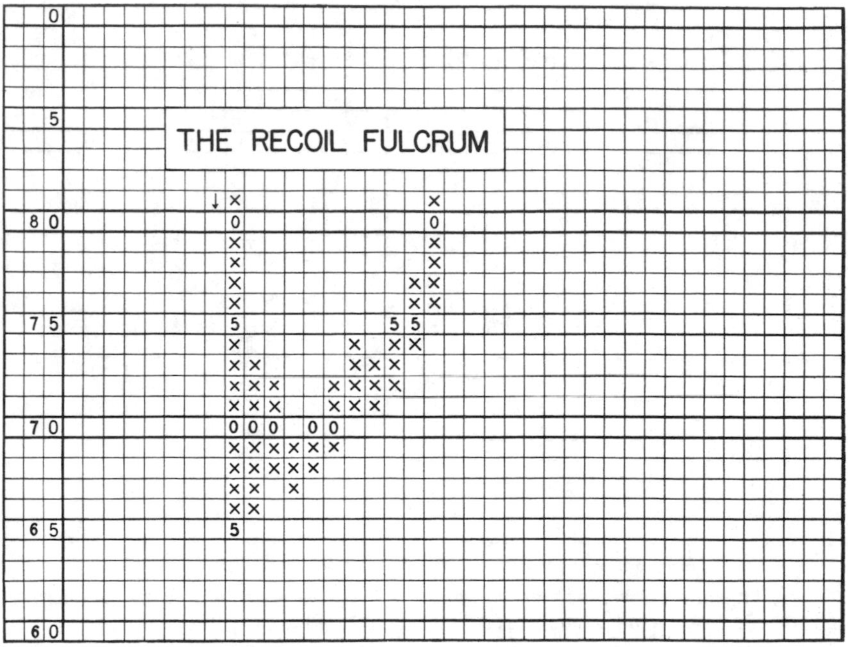

```
    0

    5          THE  RECOIL  FULCRUM

            ↓ ×                    ×
 8 0          0                    0
              ×                    ×
              ×                    ×
              ×                  × ×
              ×                  × ×
 7 5          5                5 5
              ×          ×     × ×
            × ×        × × ×
            × × ×    × × × ×
            × × ×    × × ×
 7 0        0 0 0  0 0
            × × × × × × ×
            × × × × ×
            × ×    ×
            × ×
 6 5          5

 6 0
```

The recoil fulcrum develops subsequent to a sharp and direct down move after a base forms with ascending bottoms instead of flat bottoms.

FIGURE 7   The Ideal Full Fulcrum

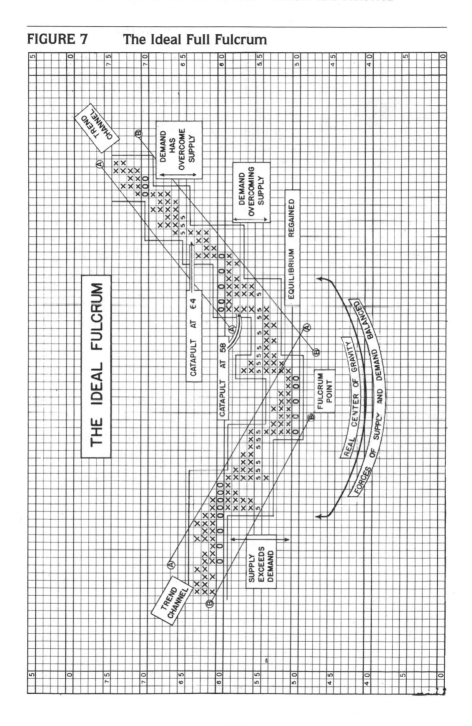

CATAPULT ACTION

The Catapult

The next important principle in the Point and Figure Method is the catapult which develops after the formation known as the full fulcrum.

The encyclopedia describes a catapult as "an ancient military engine used for hurling missiles." The word "catapult" is also defined: "to rush suddenly."

A catapult point on your Point and Figure chart is that price from which a sharp rally should develop. A catapult develops directly as the full fulcrum is completed and is that point just above the previous rally top created before the completion of the full fulcrum. Catapults are of two types: (a) the **true catapult**, (b) the **false catapult**.

The True Catapult

The true catapult (see Figure 8 on page 65) invariably develops profits without registering a reaction which would cause loss to a commitment established at that point. A minor, temporary, technical reaction from the catapult point or one or more points above the catapult position is a normal occurrence, and tolerable allowance should be made for it when establishing your position at the catapult point

The False Catapult

Occasionally, during a period of indecision and uncertainty, near the bottom of a secondary correction or near the top of a major move in a bull market, a new high level above previous highs will be established, and either a false catapult (see Figure 9 on page 66) or a semi-catapult develops. When a false catapult develops, we must be on the alert, for a stock which creates false catapults is in the act of changing its technical position. The failure of a catapult to develop profits immediately is an indication that the congestion area immediately preceding, which you may have diagnosed

FIGURE 8   The True Catapult

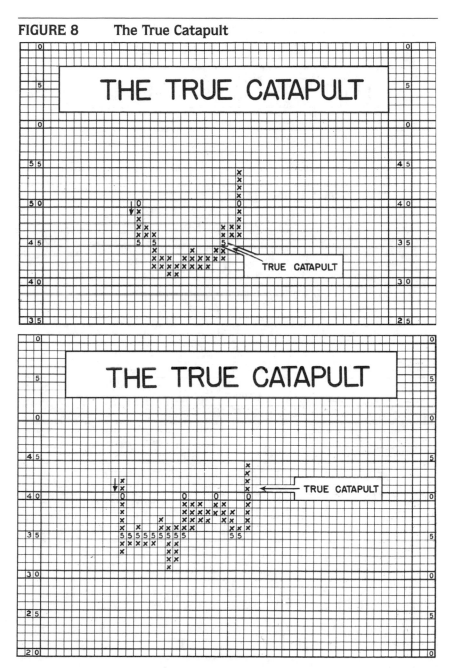

These two examples illustrate a true catapult—that point just above the previous rally top created before the completion of the full fulcrum.

FIGURE 9   The False Catapult

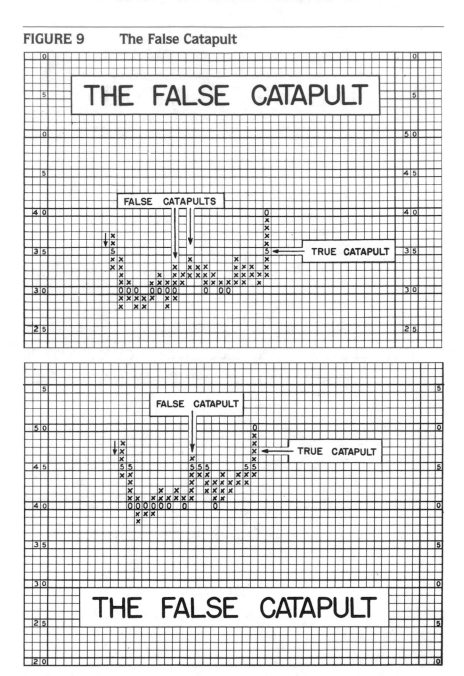

These two examples illustrate both the false catapult and the true catapult. The false catapult is a warning and indicates that the stock is in the act of changing technical positions.

to be a full ideal fulcrum, is developing into a zone of distribution and must be carefully watched lest the previous base level be violated.

In the great majority of instances, your false catapult position will permit you to close out your commitment without loss. A stock which has created a false catapult will, in many instances, come back close to that point so that you can sell out your position with but a fractional loss. This position may be protected with a "stop" below the congestion area or a "stop" just below the 50 percent reaction point after the catapult has been developed. In either case, subsequent strength should be used to move up your "stop-order" so that the failure of the position to develop into a true catapult will not cause you serious loss.

The Semi-Catapult

In addition to the two important points for establishing commitments, namely: (1) in the base of the full fulcrum, (2) at the full catapult point; there develops a third which is known as a **semi-catapult** position.

The semi-catapult position develops **during an advance** in stock as a result of a minor, narrow and limited trading range congestion area usually built up on your Point and Figure charts and from which a stock has a minor technical correction. A semi-catapult point, in this instance, develops after a technical setback when the stock rallies and creates a new high above the immediate preceding congestion area top. There are both **true** (see Figure 10 on page 68) and **false** (see Figure 11 on page 69) semi-catapults which develop in the price progression.

Use "Stops" to Protect Position

The semi-catapult position is the third important point at which to place your commitment. It usually develops profits quickly for you. The proper place for "stop-order" protection on this commitment would be below the low made during the technical correction. After strength develops, the "stop" thus placed below the technical reaction level should be advanced to an "at the flat" position, thereby insuring the commitment against loss.

FIGURE 10   The True Semi-Catapult

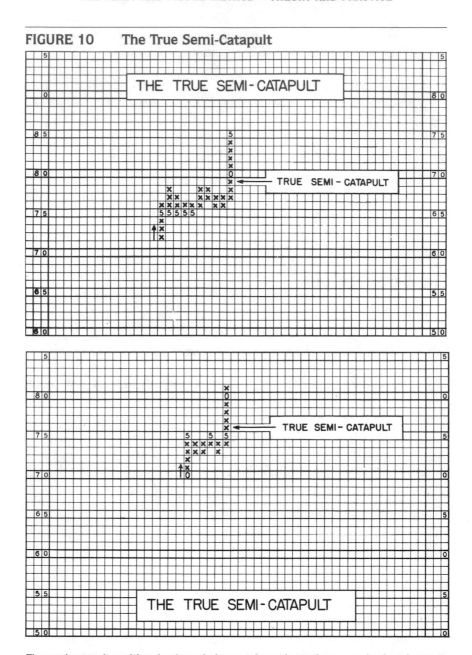

The semi-catapult position develops *during an advance* in stock as a result of a minor, narrow and limited trading range congestion area usually built up on your Point and Figure charts and from which a stock has a minor technical correction. In the true semi-catapult, the stock continues with an upward advance.

FIGURE 11   The False Semi-Catapult

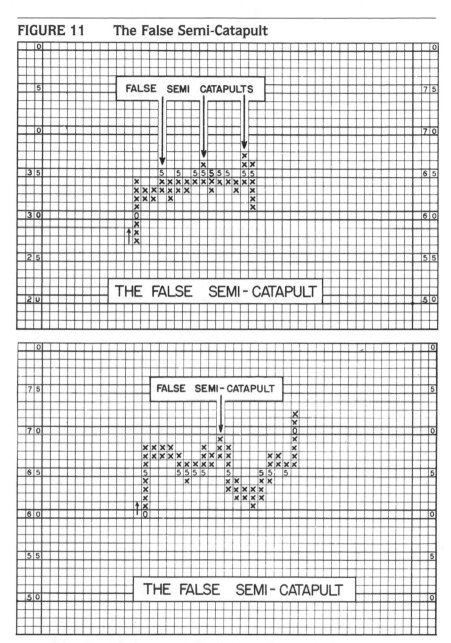

A semi-catapult point develops after a technical setback when the stock rallies and creates a new high above the immediate preceding congestion area top. When a false semi-catapult develops, as shown in the above examples, the stock price declines instead of continuing upward in its advance.

69

VII

The Principles of Charting

For the purpose of giving you a clear understanding of the plan by which the charts are made according to the Point and Figure Method, and illustrating the coordination of the one with the three point or the one with the three and five-point charts, we show an hypothetical move in the common stock of the XYZ corporation (see Figures 12, 13, and 14).

The One-Point Chart

The chart XYZ Figure 12 (see page 72) is a one-point chart illustrating a theoretical move of the common stock of the XYZ corporation. The first full-figure change shown on that chart is the symbol "5" recorded at the top of the first vertical column. This indicates that the stock sold at 25 or between 25 and 25⅞, both inclusive, on the first day in January.

In order to indicate that this was the first full figure in the month of January, instead of using the symbol "5," we substitute therefor the symbol "J." "J" indicates that this transaction is the first full-figure transaction to be recorded in the month of January. You will note, also, that we have added the year 1933 at the bottom of the column.

From the level of 25, the stock sells down to 21, or fractionally lower, but not below 20⅛, before it rallies. This calls for symbols in the squares representing 24, 23, 22 and 21. From the low on this reaction, the stock rallies and makes 24, or fractionally higher, but not above 24⅞, before

71

FIGURE 12   XYZ One-Point Chart

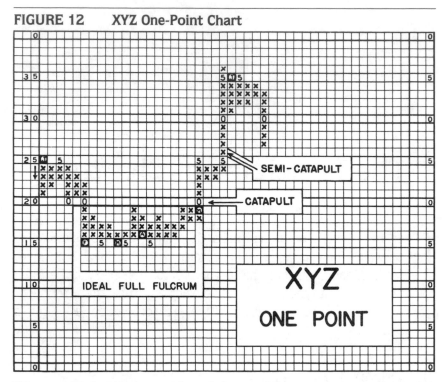

This one-point chart illustrates a theoretical move of the common stock of the the XYZ Corporation. Note the fulcrum formation as well as the full catapult and semi-catapult position indicated by arrows.

a reversal is recorded. Therefore, to plot the rally, we put the symbol "x" in the squares for 22, 23 and 24.

Move to Next Column

Note, here, that the rally requires moving over to the next right-hand column, because the square 22, in which we were to place the symbol "x" was already occupied, and we move over to the second vertical column. We proceed to plot 22, 23 and 24, and then a one-point reversal calls for a symbol in the 23 square, which, being already occupied, requires us to move once more to the next right-hand column. Moving up, we place a symbol "x" in the 24 square, and the symbol "5" in the 25 square. Then weakness develops which is stopped at 20, or above the flat figure 19.

This requires symbols to be placed in the 24, 23, 22, 21 and 20 squares. In the 20 square, we place the symbol "0" as indicated on the chart. From 20, a rally develops to 23 and a fraction, requiring symbols in the 21, 22 and 23 squares. Thereafter, further pressure develops and a reaction during the latter part of the month carries XYZ down to 15. We place symbols in the 22 and 21 squares, a zero in the 20 square, "x's" in the 19, 18, 17 and 16 squares, and since the full figure 15, is registered on the first day of February, we use the symbol "F" to show that the full figure 15, was the first full figure registered in the month of February. A rally then develops to 18, which is plotted as indicated; a reaction to 15, plotted as shown; another rally to 17; a reaction to 15, which is the first full-figure change registered in the month of March; a rally to 16; a reaction to 15; and then a sharp short covering rally to 19.

Signs of a Fulcrum

Here we have the first indication that a fulcrum is forming since the congestion area has moved the pattern over to the upper trend channel line. A short covering rally carrying the stock to 19, meets the requirements of our ideal fulcrum formation. After the rally, a sell-off carries the stock back down to 16, rally to 17, reaction to 15, rally to 18, reaction to 16, rally to 17, reaction to 16, rally to 19, reaction to 18, rally to 19, reaction to 18, and then a rally establishing a full catapult position at 20, which promptly carries through to 25. Here develops a minor technical reaction to 23, a rally to 24, reaction to 23 and another rally establishing another full catapult position at 26. The stock now rallies sharply from the full catapult at 26, until it makes a high of 36, for the move. Then there is a reaction to 31, a rally to 35, reaction to 32, a rally to 34, and then a reaction to 27. These moves are clearly illustrated on the one-point chart, Figure 12, which we ask you to study carefully.

Technical Aids

In addition to the symbols, "x," "5," and "0," we use the first letter of each month to show the first whole figure recorded in that month. Dividend payments and ex-dividend dates are registered by plotting a circle to encompass the first full figure registered on or after the ex-dividend date. When the stock sells in a zero square, on or after the ex-dividend date, instead of using a circle to encompass the square, which might complicate matters, we use a dash in the center of the zero symbol used to indicate the multiplies of tens on our charts. In addition to indicating dividend payments with the circle and dash, we make a memorandum at the foot of the column to show the amount of the dividend paid, and the date the stock sells ex-dividend. This principle of indicating dividend payments and dates is not illustrated on our theoretical charts, but it will be found on other charts contained in this book.

Examine carefully this one-point chart of XYZ (see page 72) which we used to illustrate the move and which we have traced with you. Note the fulcrum formation as well as the full catapult position indicated by arrows.

We shall proceed to show you how a three-point condensation chart is compiled from the one-point record just completed.

The Three-Point Chart

Take the three-point chart of XYZ, Figure 13 (see page 75), and compare it with the one-point chart, Figure 12 (see page 72). Let us trace the move. The three-point chart starts with the first full figure 25, records the reaction as noted on the one-point chart down to 21, as well as the rally to 24. The three-point chart disregards the reaction to 23, but when the rally from 23, to 25, registers 25, the three-point chart properly shows the move by adding a 5, above the 24 square already recorded.

The next move which is transferred to the three-point chart is the reaction down to 20, followed by the rally to 23, and then the reaction down to 15, because each of these moves is three points or more. Since the rally to 18, is three or more full points, we show it on our three-point chart and plot the move 16, 17, 18. This is followed by a decline to 15, again, which is also plotted. Then comes a series of minor rallies and declines less than three points in extent which are ignored by our three-point technic.

FIGURE 13   XYZ Three-Point Chart

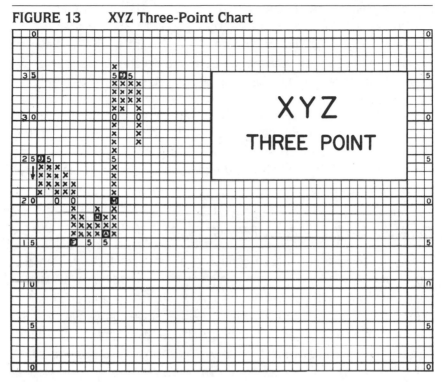

This illustrates the same move of the common stock of the the XYZ Corporation as the one in Figure 12 on page 72. Note that on the three-point chart, only rallies or declines which are of three or more full points in extent are plotted.

The next move of importance which is plotted on the three-point chart is the rally which terminates at the figure 19. Notice that we plot 16, 17, 18, and 19. The reaction from 19, to 16, is also plotted on the three-point chart, but the subsequent rally to 17, is disregarded. Where the reaction from 17, to 15, occurs, the fact that the 15, is lower than the 16, plotted on the three-point chart causes us to add the 5, below the last 16, recorded. The rally from 15, to 18, being three or more points in extent, is plotted and we add the squares 16, 17, and 18. There follows, then, a decline to 16, a rally to 17, another decline to 16, all of which are disregarded until the subsequent rally to 19. This requires that we put an "x" above the previously recorded 18, and our three-point chart now shows a rally from 15, up to 19. The minor rallies and declines of

75

one point from 19, to 18, and up to 19, down to 18, up to 19, again are all disregarded. However, the move from 18, up to 25, is plotted on the three-point chart, but the reaction on the one point from 25, down to 23, rally to 24, the next reaction to 23, all are disregarded, and the next move which carries through the catapult point to 36, is plotted.

The decline to 31, is recorded, likewise the rally to 35, also the decline to 32, but the rally to 34, being less than three points, is ignored. The decline which follows carries down to 27, requiring on our three-point chart the added figures of the last decline calling for symbols in the 31, 30, 29, 28, and 27 squares.

Determining Three-Point Moves

Thus you have learned that in compiling a three-point chart from the moves already recorded on your one-point chart, we plot on the three-point chart only rallies or declines which are of three or more full points in extent. In order to determine which are the moves to use, we consider the last recorded figure as zero, and count one, two, three. If the move carries to the third square or further, we record it. If it is less than three full figures away from the previous point recorded, it is ignored. Notice, also, a move which carries beyond the previous recorded point in the same direction is carried forward when a further move of one point or more past the previous high or low price is registered on the one-point chart.

The principle involved is as follows:
> Record all moves of three or more points in extent. Disregard reactions or reversals of less than three points. Continue the previous recorded direction by one-point plottings as soon as the price exceeds the previous low or high.

Three-point charts, in addition to their function of general condensation, form the basis for analysis of the more volatile, highly speculative, medium and high priced issues, and for the broader swings of the market. Three-point charts also show the worthwhile intermediate trend swings, because they eliminate all minor technical corrections.

The Use of Five-Point Charts

Five-point charts are used to indicate broad zones of accumulation and distribution in the main trend when plotting the market indices, and are used as basic condensation charts for the more volatile issues which move 10, 20, or 30 points in a single speculative cycle. Five-point charts condense the time factor and show long-term accumulation and distribution, and are invaluable guides to the Capital Movement Trends.

Turn, now, to Figure 14, five-point chart of "XYZ." Notice, here, that we plot from the **one-point data** only those moves which are of 5 or more points extent. A stock must rally or decline to the fifth from the last recorded square before our five-point chart records a reversal.

FIGURE 14   XYZ Five-Point Chart

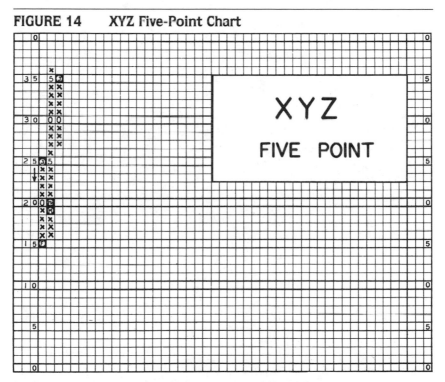

Compare this five-point chart of XYZ with your one-point chart Figure 12 on page 72 and note how this method provided a highly efficient condensation of the time factor. We plot from the *one-point data* only those moves which are of 5 or more points extent.

Nevertheless, a continuation of the move in the already plotted direction is recorded by one-point additions until a full five-point reversal occurs. In making five-point charts, we determine whether or not the move is plotted by starting to count zero at the last recorded square, then if the move is to or beyond the fifth square, it is plotted.

Compare your five-point chart of XYZ Figure 14 (see page 77) with your one-point chart Figure 12 (see page 72) and note how this Method provided a highly efficient condensation of the time factor.

VIII

Analyzing Technical Position

After you have gained a comprehensive understanding of the Method and the technic of making the charts, the next step is to study the formations as they develop, and then to classify and analyze them. It is important to know whether a stock is under accumulation in a strong technical position, under distribution in a weak technical position, or merely in an indeterminate neutral position.

The Price Path Characteristics

In studying the movements of stocks, it is well to have in mind the old saying, "Stocks must fluctuate." Price paths on your one-point charts will develop patterns that reflect the peculiar characteristics of each stock. You will begin to observe that a given advance in a certain issue is usually followed by a definite type of technical correction. You will be amazed to observe the harmonious rhythm with which certain types of issues advance or decline, and which generally repeat themselves in the price progression path. While some stocks move harmoniously, other issues are very erratic with sharp advances followed by equally short declines, and thus complete their technical correction.

Patterns of the Leaders Duplicated in the Secondary Issues

You will note, again and again, that the key issue in any group develops its characteristic pattern, which is usually duplicated by the secondary issues

79

in the same group. A catapult developing in the leader of the group one day will more than likely be followed by a similar formation in the secondary issues soon thereafter. Study carefully the number of points advance and the correction area which follows. Learn whether the correction area is a reaction of 50 or more percent of the advance or a congestion area in which the stock fluctuates back and forth while it is consolidating the move. The first correction which is greater in proportion to the last advance than the previous corrections which occurred during the advance is the first sign of distribution. Watch carefully for the first more than normal reaction.

Solid Formations Give Confidence

During an advance, we prefer to see fairly solid congestion areas after each mark-up. This indicates each stage of the advance to be well consolidated before the next up move develops. When the progression of the move proceeds with only normal and minor technical reactions, it is an indication that the technical condition of the stock continues strong. If the formations are irregular and confusing, with no uniformity of pattern, we suggest caution. It is an indication of conflict and uncertainty. Such formations, during a major advance, give rise to hollow spaces similar to air chambers beneath the congestion points. These occur as the technical corrections overextend themselves and create intervening blank spaces in the form of arched ellipses, semi-circles or irregular hollow patterns. Such formations are usually advance warnings of stubborn resistance to the advance and indicate supply meeting demand at the higher levels, with a strong possibility of a change of trend forthcoming. This indication developing on the three-point chart is particularly indicative of the imminence of a reversal in trend.

Watch for Changes in Activity

You will observe from your charts that stocks fluctuate narrowly during periods of major accumulation. Soon thereafter, activity, sharp advances and equally sharp technical declines follow. This is usually a sign of the beginning of an extended move. Watch carefully for it. When a stock alters its most recent fluctuating habits, it is wise to be on the alert, for it is a sign of either accumulation or distribution.

Strong and Weak Technical Position

The technical position of a stock or the market, as represented by an index, is strong when demand exceeds supply. This condition develops after a period of accumulation which has followed a major decline. A strong technical condition also exists after a mark-up followed by a congestion area which develops to be consolidation.

When stock is purchased and taken out of the floating supply, technical condition is very strong. As a stock develops a strong technical position, the one-point charts should show an extended line of work in the congestion area, either with a well-formed, fairly solid, flat base, or a series of bases like a descending stairway, the bottom base containing the greatest number of squares along the support line. This type of base occurs very often. An exceedingly strong base develops after a sharp decline when each successive rally and decline builds up a triangle with its vertex to the right. When this formation develops to be accumulation, an extremely strong technical position exists.

Weak Technical Position

A weak technical position develops after a series of extended advances which are uncorrected by congestion areas of consolidation. As the move progresses, the advances are not as vigorous as the early ones, and soon the ascending move begins to give way to a series of confused and halting patterns created by the churning motion near the top, which you will recognize as distribution. This formation occurs when supply begins to overcome demand.

At this point, it is important to check against your three-point charts in order to observe the consolidated moves and to judge whether or not a real ceiling, which is apt to precede a drastic reversal, has been formed. Should this formation near the top of an extended move begin to develop reactions which leave air pockets, arched ellipses and other hollow areas beneath the congestion zone, it is an ominous sign and time to close out the position or to protect it by close stops.

Gauging the Length and Culmination of the Moves

For the more advanced students and technicians, the Point and Figure Method affords a purely mechanical means of judging the length and culmination of future moves. This system, although not absolutely accurate, is extremely helpful in judging the proper moment to close out a position. It is truly mechanical and involves little judgment to make it operative.

The Count

This system, an individual characteristic of the Point and Figure Method, is popularly known as "the count" to students and technicians. Because of the fact that it is somewhat involved and requires a lengthy explanation with multitudinous concrete examples and considerable study before it can be understood, it is omitted from this volume and will be found in the more advanced work entitled *The Advanced Theory and Practice of the Point and Figure Method*, by the same authors.

Coordinating Your Studies

We have stated that it is vitally important to record the action of the market by plotting the important and popular indices, as well as the half-hourly, half-point movements of the popular Dow Jones Industrial Index. The conclusions which you will make resulting from the study of the charts of these indices should be used to influence the opinion arrived at from the study of individual issues. It is well to remember that you buy and sell individual stocks; therefore, it is most important for you to make your commitments based upon your analysis of the individual issues, substantiating your judgment through the influences of the averages. ***Always remember that we buy and sell stocks and not index numbers.***

You have now completed a full and detailed course on the elementary principles upon which the Point and Figure Method is based. In order that you may get a clearer understanding of how to apply your knowledge of the Method, we will proceed to take you through a complete intermediate trend cycle move of several issues as illustrated in Chapters IX and X. In Chapter XI you will learn how to plot and analyze the half-point, half-hourly running index lines of the Dow Jones Industrial Averages. In Chapter XII, by aid of the Point and Figure Method five-point chart on which are plotted the moves of the New York Times index, we will show you how a knowledge and application of this Method would have avoided drastic losses which many suffered in 1929, when the last bear market had its inception. Lastly, we will take you through the campaign of Atlas Tack, illustrating to you the application of the knowledge you have acquired, and showing how such knowledge and application would have permitted you to buy and sell with the insiders and share in the sensational moves which were completed by the insiders in that campaign.

IX

Anticipating the Action of U.S. Steel

Examine chart Figure 15 (see page 87), which shows the one-point moves of U.S. Steel during the primary trend cycle of 1933.

The Full Ideal Fulcrum

Figure 15, shows all one-point moves in U.S. Steel from the first day of January 1933, up to near the close of the month of June of the same year. Charts like this are compiled from the *Full Figure Daily Data* supplied by the publishers or from the one-point moves which you may obtain from actual tape action. In the previous chapters we have shown the correct procedure for the plotting of one-point moves. Examine this chart Figure 15. Notice the congestion area between the column marked "A" and the one marked "B." You will recognize this to be an ideal full fulcrum, which meets almost exactly the requirements as laid down in the definition for this type of formation. The first column indicates an up move starting with the first day in January, after which the action proceeds with its backing and filling until the low point was reached, and which was established before the fourth of March, when President Roosevelt was inaugurated. The rally to full figure 33, was created after the bank holiday, when the market opened up sharply and exceptional strength developed. The subsequent correction which carried down to full figure 27, was completed later in March. In April the stock began to develop new strength and a sharp up trend was recorded with ascending bottoms.

The Catapult Position

Notice that the pattern from the beginning of the year until the column marked "B" indicated the required down trend, the first rally followed by a technical correction which holds above the previous base level and then a succeeding rally which develops a catapult point, both of which are indicative of a trend reversal. Note in column "C" the full figure 34, indicated with an arrow. This is the most important of all signals given by the Point and Figure Method. It is a full true catapult point. Observe that ten points quick profit develops after a position is established at this point. An order placed to "Buy U.S. Steel on stop at 34," would show ten points quick profit without registering even a small paper loss.

The Semi-Catapult Position

The congestion area which begins to register in the column "D" and carries forward to the column "E" is a temporary halting of the up trend. It is the type of congestion area which develops a semi-catapult point. In column "F," full figure 45, develops to be the semi-catapult point and substantial profits accrue to this position without subsequently showing any loss to a position thus established. While the move from 45, was not as spectacular as the one from 34, nevertheless, it developed more than 18 points profit before the end of the move was completed.

Consolidating the Gains

Note the one-point decline and subsequent rally plotted in column "G." Here is indicated a temporary supply of stock at the 49 level, which is blocking further advance. The stock reacts from 49, to 47, rallies again to 49, and then reacts to 46, in column "H." Column "I" shows good buying around the 46 level because the second decline fails to go lower and creates a double bottom at 46. Thereafter, the stock develops strength, and in column "J," a new semi-catapult develops. A reaction follows, in column "K." In column "L," it goes through to new high ground forming a new semi-catapult at 51. A small reaction then follows and in column "M" a new semi-catapult develops at 52. Now you will begin to notice that in the upper 50 zone the stock is meeting definite resistance. The moves are

FIGURE 15   U.S. Steel One-Point Chart (1 of 2)

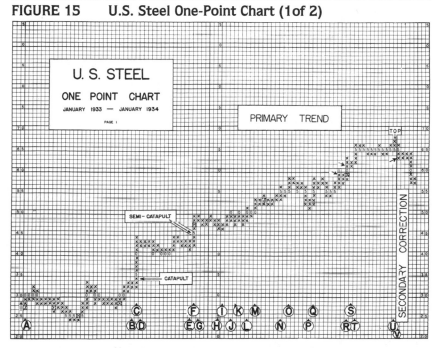

This chart shows the one-point moves of U.S. Steel during the primary trend cycle of 1933. Note in column "C" the full figure 34, indicated with an arrow. This is a full true catapult point, the most important of all signals given by the Point and Figure Method. Also notice the arrows pointing to the semi-catapult positions at full figure 45, 59, and 61. In column "U" we see another two arrows pointing to a ceiling or fulcum in reverse and a reverse catapult position at point 63. The reverse fulcum indicates the end of a move.

not nearly as sharp as they were previous to this point, and the progress, though it goes somewhat higher to approximately 65 or 66, is made with great effort and with many rallies and declines. New semi-catapults are developed in column "N" at 55, and in column "O" at 57, when a rally to 58 meets strong resistance and develops a double top, after which the first extensive reaction is witnessed which carries the stock in column "P" back down to the 51 level.

The Final Mark Up

Here a sharp recovery takes place which is plotted in column "Q." Such a sharp recovery from a low of 51, indicates technical strength. The reaction from 58, down to 56, is another bullish implication because it is a normal correction. Then the stock rallies back to 58 making a quadruple top at this point. The subsequent decline to 54, where another double bottom is established, is bullish because it holds substantially above the previously recorded low point at 51. New semi-catapults develop at 59, and at 61.

The End of the Move —A Reverse Fulcrum

Figure 16, shows the continuation of the move of U.S. Steel which was carried forward from the point left off in Figure 15 on the previous page. Notice the congestion area which builds up around 65, and note further

---

FIGURE 16　　U.S. Steel One-Point Chart (2 of 2)

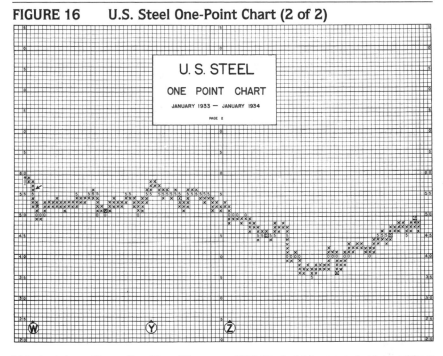

This chart shows the continuation of the move of U.S. Steel which was carried forward from the point left off in Figure 15 on the previous page. In column "W" at 56, a reverse semi-catapult position develops, and the profits of a down move quickly accrue. The extended congestion area plotted between the columns "W" and "Z" is an indication of a close balancing of the forces of supply and demand.

that for the first time we have a quintuple top and a failure to carry through the resistance level at 66 and 67. The actual top of this move is plotted and indicated by the arrow at 67. Here is the end of the primary bull trend of U.S. Steel in 1933.

The Short Positions

From this point forward, the secondary correction commences, and we see between columns "T," and "V," the congestion area known as a ceiling or fulcrum in reverse with its top point plotted in column "U" and the reverse catapult position at 63, indicated by an arrow, in column "U" (see Figure 15 on page 87) In column "W" at 56, a reverse semi-catapult position develops, and the profits of a down move quickly accrue. Examine, now, the extended congestion area plotted between the columns "W" and "Z." Here you see an indication of a close balancing of the forces of supply and demand. In column "Y," the failure of the rally to carry further is an indication of developing weakness. Notice the down trend which develops soon thereafter (see Figure 16 on page 88).

Geometrical Charts

In order that you may have an understanding of the application of the one-point geometrical chart, we have plotted a part of the one-point moves of U.S. Steel by geometrical technic. This is illustrated in Figure 17 (see page 90). Examine it carefully and compare it with the one-point chart and with vertical line bar charts of the same move. This will give you a clear illustration of the advantage to be gained from the application of the Point and Figure Method to stock price movements.

The Trend Outline Charts

In Figure 18 (see page 90), we show the plotting of a trend outline chart of the three-point moves of U.S. Steel. These charts, while not necessary in a technical analysis, are sometimes very helpful to students who will take the time to draw them.

FIGURE 17   U.S. Steel One-Point Geometric Chart

This chart shows the one-point moves of U.S. Steel Figure 15 plotted by geometric technic.

FIGURE 18   U.S. Steel Three-Point Trend Outline Chart

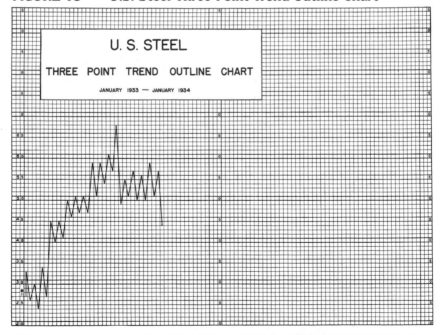

This chart shows a trend outline of the three-point moves of U.S. Steel from Figure 19.

The Three-Point Figure Charts

Figure 19, is a three-point condensation chart compiled from the one-point data of Figures 15 and 16, and shows the moves of U.S. Steel from the beginning of the year 1933, up to the end of September of the same year. Notice how the catapults and the semi-catapults develop on the three-point chart and how they confirm the conclusions arrived at through the study of your one-point charts. One should always compile a three-point chart for every one-point chart that he keeps. One- and three-point charts are vital and essential to a proper application of the principles of this Method.

FIGURE 19   U.S. Steel Three-Point Chart

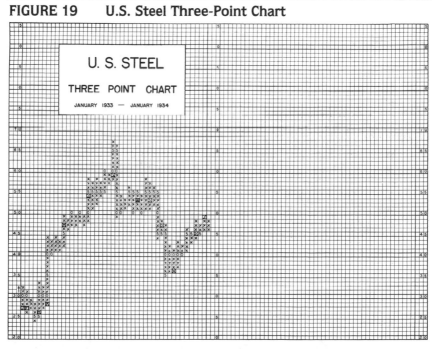

This is a three-point condensation chart compiled from the one-point data of Figures 15 and 16 on pages 87 and 88. It shows the moves of U.S. Steel from the beginning of the year 1933, up to the end of September of the same year. Notice how the catapults and the semi-catapults develop on the three-point chart and how they confirm the conclusions arrived at through the study of your one-point charts.

The Five-Point Charts

In Figure 20, we show the five-point moves of U.S. Steel. The five-point data is obtained from the one-point charts Figures 15, and 16. Five-point charts are very helpful and show the broader zones of accumulation and distribution. They should always be compiled to show the moves of the main indexes and the volatile issues.

Summary

When you attempt to establish a long position near the base of a fulcrum, your stop must be placed very close. Your position established at the cata-pult point must allow for a 50 percent correction of the last advance. The

---

FIGURE 20   U.S. Steel Five-Point Chart

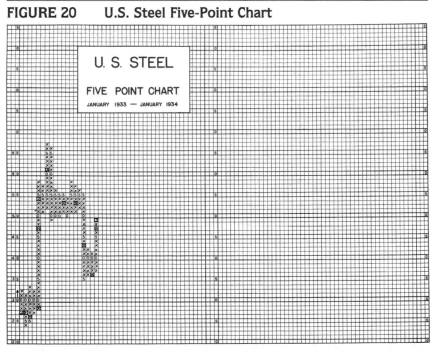

The five-point data is obtained from the one-point charts Figures 15 and 16 on pages 87 and 88. Five-point charts are very helpful and show the broader zones of accumulation and distribution.

same is true for the semi-catapult points. Note that the further the move has extended itself from the full fulcrum base, the more dangerous it is to establish a long position. After an extended advance, you run the risk of a more than normal technical correction touching off your stop. Be patient. Before you establish your position wait for the terminations of secondary corrections in a bull market. Analyze your formations carefully; then proceed with confidence as the full fulcrums and catapults develop.

X

Analyzing a Campaign in Western Union

O ne of the most widely known multi-millionaire stock market operators, who lived and prospered at the turn of the last century, used to counsel his friends to buy Western Union Common whenever it was available around $50 a share. Western Union Common has a $100 par value and formerly paid an $8 annual dividend. It was considered one of the prime blue chips. In the 1929 bull market, Western Union sold above $270 per share. In 1932, at the bear market low, its price registered $12.375. Hundreds of thousands of shares were turned over at price levels far below $50, which was the level at which the older generation of authorities counseled their friends to buy. It sold at one-quarter that price at the bear market low.

Selecting the Fast Moving Issues

In 1933, a remarkable campaign developed in this issue. It began around the end of February, or the beginning of March as shown on the chart, Figure 21 (see page 96). The stock was available between $18 and $20 a share for many days during February, March and April. In a very few weeks it advanced sharply and in a spectacular manner from the level of 18, to more than $75 per share. Here you have a move with a possibility of more than 300 percent profit, since $1800 invested in 100 shares of this stock would have grown to $7500 in a short time. Notwithstanding such a tremendous profit percentage, there was nothing about the move which was not clearly indicated on the charts. You too could have had your share of those profits which were made by many who understood the technical condition of this issue. Your one- and three-point charts indicated the move weeks in advance.

The Full Fulcrum Base

Figure 21, is a one-point chart of Western Union. Observe that the down move was arrested near the end of February and the beginning of March and how a congestion area base with a flat bottom was built up between full figure 18 and 20. Note the sharp rally in the middle of the fulcrum when the stock advanced to 27, in one sharp, rapid upsurge from the low of 18. Here was a sign of technical strength, a 50 percent advance

FIGURE 21   Western Union One-Point Chart (1 of 2)

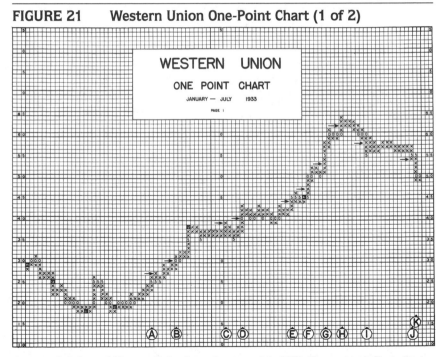

A one-point chart of Western Union from January - July 1933. The arrows indicate buying levels at point 27, the first full fulcrum position, and at semi-catapults points 30, 39, 40, 44, 47, 53, and 62. The stock has advanced from 18 to 64 without a worthwhile technical set-back. The beginning of a correction is indicated by the reverse fulcrum in column "H" followed by a reverse semi-catapult at full figure 54 in column "J."

in the price of that stock within one day's market action. Surely no one could have failed to recognize such a definite signal. Its confirmation was had after the correction which held firmly in a double bottom formation established at 18, near the end of March and the beginning of April. Here a new base builds up at a somewhat higher level and the formation begins to meet the requirements of the ideal full fulcrum. In column "A," when the stock has advanced to 26, this fulcrum is completed. The arrow in the next adjoining right-hand column pointing at full figure 27 shows the first full catapult position.

The Catapult

Take particular notice of the firm and definite up trend which the issue establishes as it advances from 20, up through the catapult point and establishes another semi-catapult position at 30. This sharp up trend and its angle of inclination is a confirmation of the strength indicated in mid-March and connotes sharp continuation of the up trend soon to come. The advance begins to develop in column "B" from the semi-catapult point at 30. The stock soon rallies sharply to 38.

The Semi-Catapults

A new semi-catapult position is developed at full figure 39, in column "C." Then follows a minor technical correction and a rally which establishes a new semi-catapult position at full figure 40, shown at the arrow point in column "D." The congestion area terminating with column "D," shows an excellent solid consolidation of the advance with the stock reestablishing a strong technical position and indicating a further sharp up move soon to follow. The rallies and declines between column "D" and column "E" create further consolidation, establish additional strength, and create a new semi-catapult at 44, shown in column "E." Another semi-catapult is shown in column "F," and still another in column "G." Notice how sharply the stock now advances. An additional semi-catapult position is shown at 62 in column "H." Here one must be on guard. The stock has advanced from 18 to 64, shown on Chart Figure 21, without a worthwhile technical setback. Proceed, now, to Chart Figure 22 (see page 98). Observe that the correction sets in.

FIGURE 22   Western Union One-Point Chart (2 of 2)

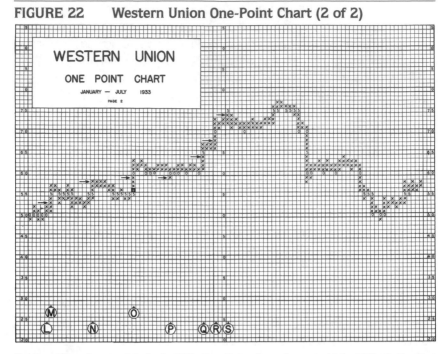

Continuation of one-point chart of Western Union from January - July 1933. Notice that the correction sets in. The development of the ideal full fulcrum in column "L" is a sign of developing strength, and an indication of the termination of an intermediate swing. From the base at 49 to 50 the stock has again had a 25-point advance when it establishes a semi-catapult position at 74, in column "S." Note that the congestion area to the right of column "S" is a sign of developing weakness and you should be on guard.

The Short Positions

A reverse fulcrum develops with a short position catapult indication at 58. This is indicated with an arrow in column "I." A reverse semi-catapult develops at 54, indicated in column "J." After the down move in column "K," notice the congestion area that builds up between the columns "K" and "L." This is an ideal full fulcrum, always a sign of developing strength, and an indication of the termination of an intermediate swing. It is always a signal to go long of the stock at the next catapult point. A catapult develops at full figure 53, indicated in column "M." Profits soon accrue as the stock rallies to 57 and a fraction. Some little resistance is met at that point, and the stock makes a double top at 57, after which it sells down

98

to 53. In the zones between columns "M" and "N," one would be justified in being somewhat hesitant and in doubt about the technical position. The formation is a neutral one until a double bottom is established at 52. The decline which establishes the first 52, creates a new low after the 53, previously recorded and is to be considered a cautionary sign. However, when the stock rallies in column "N" and creates a new semi-catapult at 58, we have an indication of new strength developing. Notice the semi-catapult which is built up between column "N" and column "O," with its miniature full fulcrum at the bottom. Again an excellent semi-catapult position is built up at full figure 59, indicated with the arrow in column "O." The stock continues its advance, but meets with some difficulty, however, between zones the of 60 and 63. When it establishes a new low at 59, indicated in column "P," we must be on guard.

Any position now established must be stopped close beneath the low made on the move which was recorded at full figure 64. The zone from column "O," to column "Q." is a congestion area, of the type which sometimes develops to be the culmination of the move. Be on guard, however, when the stock develops a new semi-catapult at 64, in column "Q." It is a sign of strength. Congestion zone between "Q," and "R," is a consolidation of the gain, and a new semi-catapult position is established in column "R" at the 68 point.

From the base at 49 to 50 the stock has again had a 25-point advance when it establishes a semi-catapult position at 74, in column "S." The congestion area to the right of column "S" is a sign of developing weakness. Be on guard and ready to take your profits on further strength or when subsequent weakness reaches your stop order which should be advanced beneath the market as the move progresses upward.

Summary

We are sure, that from a study of the one-point moves in Western Union you would have been able to detect and take advantage of an exceptional campaign without the aid of tips, rumors or boardroom gossip. Examine your three-point condensation chart Figure 23 (see page 100). Notice how readily these two types of charts are used in conjunction with each

FIGURE 23   Western Union Three-Point Chart

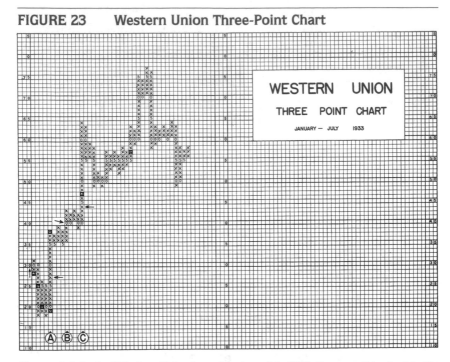

Three-point chart of Western Union from January - July 1933. Compare this chart to the one-point charts of Western Union on pages 96 and 98. Notice the indicated buying levels on your one-point charts as they develop confirmations (shown by the arrows in columns "A," "B," and "C") on the above three-point chart.

other. See the indicated buying levels on your one-point charts as they develop confirmations on your three-point charts. We show them with arrows in columns "A," "B," and "C," in Figure 23. Compare them with Figures 21 (see page 96) and 22 (see page 98). From these charts you will learn that it is not necessary for you to listen to tips or rumors which circulate about the boardrooms and are printed in many of your daily financial publications.

Study well and master the principles of this time-tried Method and you will always be able to anticipate stock price movements weeks before the tips and rumors filter their way into the boardrooms and financial columns.

XI

Judging the Minor Swings

E
lsewhere in the book, we have promised to give you the details and explain the methods used in compiling a ***running action index line***, which is considered a vital aid by most experienced market technicians.

The Half-Hourly Index of the Dow Jones Industrials

For the purpose of judging the day-to-day minor swings of the market, there is no technical aid as helpful as a one-half point figure chart of the half-hourly position of the Dow Jones Industrial Index.

For the purpose of facilitating the plotting of the action of this running line we have especially designed a one-half point chart sheet known as #5001.5. Students of the Method will find this sheet ideal for the purpose.

Messrs. Dow Jones and Company have recently inaugurated the policy of publishing the hourly position of their Dow Jones Industrial Index. Since the fall of 1931, your authors have privately compiled this important index at each half-hour interval during every trading day. These computations form the basis for this exceedingly helpful half-point half-hourly index. The data for carrying this chart forward is supplied in the *Full Figure Daily Data Service* available from the publishers. This most indispensable index represents the fluctuations of the market as it actually moves from point to point during the day. Notice that the maximum high established in the newspapers and the maximum low are disregarded when we use a running action index line. We are concerned only with the fluctuations of the index as it moves in a continuous line throughout the day, and from day to day. The total of the maximum highs of the stocks which comprise the index highs, or the maximum lows which comprise the index lows, does not interest us.

We are concerned only with the relative strength or weakness of the rallies and declines as they develop and with the resultant congestion areas built up as the index line fluctuates during each market session. Of course, knowledge of the maximum high, the maximum low, and the close of each day is helpful in judging the technical position of the market; but more important for the technician is the information which is to be had from starting and maintaining this important half-point half-hourly running line index of the Dow Jones Industrial averages.

The Half-Point Half-Hourly Log

Turn now to Figure 24 (see page 103). The half-point figure chart plotted here for you represents the technical action of the market, and, as continued on Figure 25 (See page 104), shows the action from the beginning of the year 1933, to beyond the top established in July. The chart terminates with the action indicated about the middle of August at the right-hand edge of Figure 25.

Half-Point Technic

Observe, here, that half-point technic is exactly like your one-point technic, the only difference being that the crossing of the halfway zone and the full-figure zone calls for a new symbol. Thus, a move from 101 to 102.56 would require "x's" in the lower half of the 101 square, in the upper half of the 101 square, in the lower half of the 102 square, and in the upper half of the 102 square, showing that the move had reached the halfway point, or beyond. Should the move carry to 102.99, no additional symbol would be needed, but the moment it registers 103, we would be required to put a symbol in the lower half square of the 103

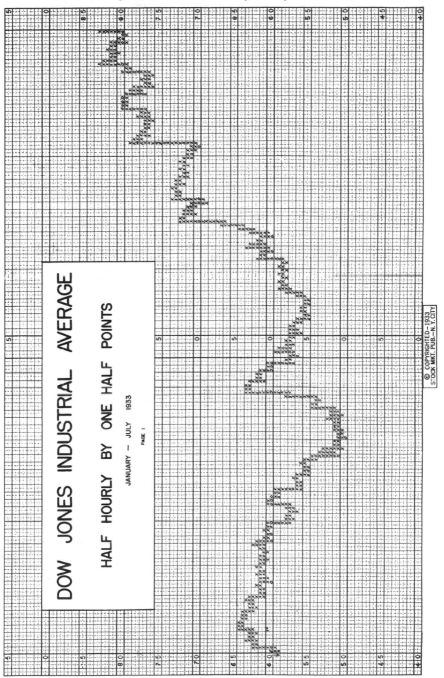

DOW JONES INDUSTRIAL AVERAGE

HALF HOURLY BY ONE HALF POINTS

JANUARY — JULY 1933

PAGE I

© COPYRIGHTED—1933
STOCK MKT. PUB.—N.Y.CITY

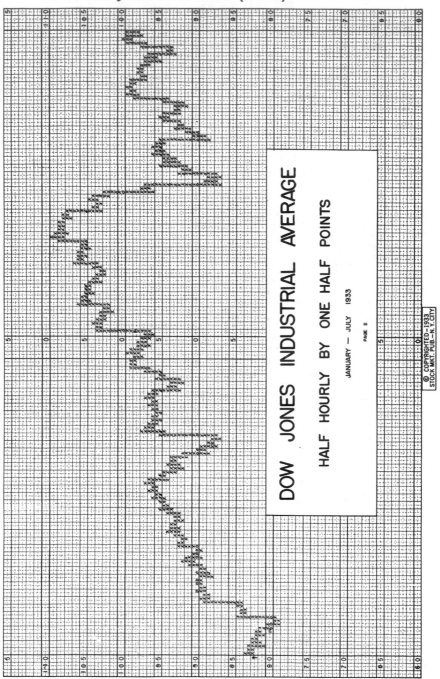

DOW JONES INDUSTRIAL AVERAGE

HALF HOURLY BY ONE HALF POINTS

JANUARY — JULY 1933

PAGE 2

© COPYRIGHTED—1933
STOCK MKT. PUB.—N. Y. CITY

level showing that 103 flat had been reached. We feel confident that you will understand the technic of developing these half-point charts, especially so if you are sure of your one-point technic.

Scientific Tape Reading

These valuable charts are very helpful to the boardroom trader and others who attempt to catch the shorter swings. They are far more reliable than an attempt at tape reading. This half-hourly running line index plotted by half points is actually a picturization of the tape itself. It is dependable and helpful. It is far more reliable than trusting to memory or hazarding a guess. We urge upon every one of our readers to establish and maintain this half-hourly log in half-point form. It is a formidable tool and invaluable as an aid in recognizing the day-to-day trend of the market. As you proceed to study half-point technic and its application to the running action line, you will begin to realize that the vital mechanical principles forming the basis of the Point and Figure Method, namely, the fulcrum, the catapult and the semi-catapult are clearly recognizable in your half-point half-hourly market log chart. Compile and maintain this chart. Watch the trend lines on it as they develop. Notice the congestion areas at the terminations of the swings as the market moves up or down the trend channel.

Analyzing the Half-Point Chart

Be on guard after a sharp upsurge when resistance to the advance is clearly indicated. Be ready to buy stocks after an extended decline when a congestion area builds up a fulcrum and a catapult develops. Consider the broader trend channels on this index to show you the trend of the market. The closer trend lines in the congestion areas will show you the danger zones after an upsurge, and the point at which to liquidate your long position. The important buying levels indicated on this chart are in the bases formed after a down move when a full fulcrum or a catapult develops. Watch closely congested zones. Also, be on the alert to take advantage of the semi-catapult position which may develop in the price progression path of this important technical aid.

Ignore Rumors and Gossip

If you maintain and study this chart you will soon be able to disregard the advice of your customers man or the boardroom habitués and the gossip in which they indulge. If, in the face of bad news and pessimism, this important half-hourly index builds up a congestion area of accumulation, disregard the bad news, ignore the rumors, establish your long position and have patience. Likewise, when all is enthusiasm and stock price advances get on to the front pages of our newspapers, your half-point chart will either be showing a clear and already effected advance or the building up of a congestion zone. Congestion zones give implications requiring caution. Be ready to liquidate quickly at first signs of a ceiling developing even though the news and all about you are rampantly optimistic.

Summary

It is well to remind you, at this time, that you cannot trade in index numbers. The half-point half-hourly running action index log is but a representation of the market. You must trade in stocks. When your index line is bullish, select the most bullish formations in individual stocks and place your position in those stocks. Use this valuable Half-Hourly Log as an aid to reinforce your judgment. From it, analyze daily, the technical position of the market.

XII

Half-Point Technic
in Atlas Tack

I n order that you may have an illustration of how the half-point, Point and Figure technic is applied to an individual issue, we shall take you through the recent campaign in Atlas Tack. The sensational advance of this low-priced stock which advanced within a few weeks from $1.50 per share to $34.75, attracted the attention of the Stock Exchange authorities and the Attorneys-General of several states.

Historical Background

The Atlas Tack Corporation was first listed on the New York Stock Exchange at the beginning of the last bull market during 1920 or 1921. There are issued and outstanding 98,000 shares of common stock of no par value. The bull market high of 1929 was 17⅞. The low of that year was 5. In the period of 1930 and 1931, the high was 8½, and the low 1½. The bear market low in 1932 was 1, and the high of that year 3⅞. In 1933, the low was 1½, the high 34¾. In the month of December 1933, the high was 34¾, and low 10.

Here was an issue which presented an ideal opportunity for unscrupulous market operators to take advantage of the public. The small outstanding capital stock, with most of the stock closely held, and an extremely small floating supply, permitted of easy manipulation.

Analyzing the Campaign in Atlas Tack

Turn, now, to the chart Figure 26 (see page 109). This is a one-half point chart showing all the one-half point changes in Atlas Tack from the high of the year 1930 to the low of the bear market and up to the high established on a recent date in 1933. Observe the zone between columns A, and D. Here you will see the type of fulcrum which will always develop in low-priced stocks when you apply half-point technic to their fluctuations. Give particular attention to that formation. Notice the difference between it and the one-point fulcrums.

The sell off in column A, from the high of 8½, was quite sharp, considering the price level. At 1½, some resistance to the decline was met as the stock was picked up by the insiders. In the zone A, to B, the stock was several years under accumulation with very few transactions being registered on the tape. Little was heard or seen of Atlas Tack during 1932. In the last quarter of the year, during the months of October, November and December, the stock sold down from 3½ to the actual low of 1¾, registered near column B. A few transactions were effected in the month of February, 1933, around the price of 1½. Later, a few thousand shares changed hands at 1¾, to 2, and in the month of April, we find a few shares changing hands during the first week of that month at $3 per share. During the month of May, the price of the stock advanced from 3 to 3½. Thus, you see, between the months of October 1932 and the end of April 1933, Atlas Tack had a very thin market while it was being accumulated by the insiders, when 7,500 shares comprised the total transactions. At 4, shown in column B, the stock was on the catapult. This was the first important buying signal.

Things began to happen during the last week of May 1933. It was at this stage, in the zone marked C to D2, that the manipulators begin to take a real interest in the issue. The advance from the bear market low to 10½, the top of the rally in column D2, is to be considered a normal one for a low-priced stock of a company with fairly good prospects of future earnings. The zone from column B, to column C, represents the final stage of accumulation, C, being the June shake-out of the 1933, bull market run-up. In column D1, we find the first semi-catapult occurring at 8½ in this issue. Another developed at 9, in column D2. These two semi-catapults were buying points.

FIGURE 26   Atlas Tack Corp. Half-Point Chart
March 1930 - January 1934

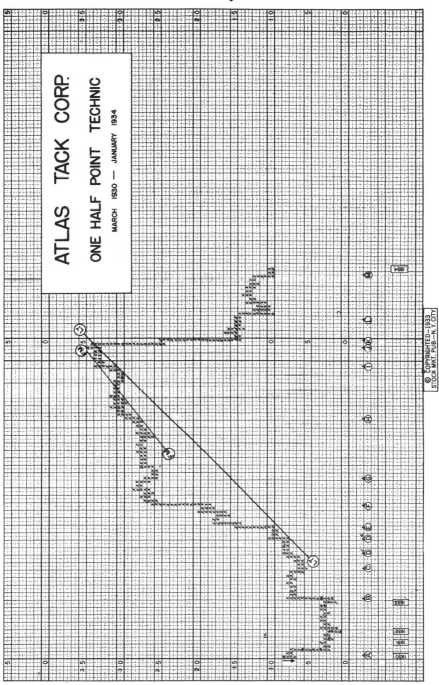

The action of Atlas Tack from the zone A to E represents a normal bull market action of a low-priced issue. Low-priced issues always have best percentage advances from a bear market low point.[6] Accumulation was effected in the zones A, to B, during the run-up in column B, and from B to D1. At the point marked E, we consider that the manipulators had completed their line and the stock formed a new semi-catapult at 11, which was another important buying signal. This took place during the month of August while the rest of the market was recovering from the drastic effects of the July break.

Important Signal During July Break

In the July break, while the rest of the market lost twenty-five percent of the average price, namely from 110.00 in the Dow Jones Industrial Index to 85.00, a net change of approximately 25 points, Atlas Tack had but a slight sell-off from 10½ to 9½, which constituted the technical reaction betweens columns D2, and E. That was an important and significant signal to the effect that big things were about to happen in Atlas Tack.

The negligible drop in the price of Atlas Tack during the July break was much less than normally would be expected and showed extremely strong sponsorship. To those who observed its action by half-point technic of the Point and Figure Method, the next semi-catapult point would have suggested an immediate purchase. Certainly, the fourth buying place, the semi-catapult at 11, would have been the best point at which to go long of this issue. The mark up in the zone column E, to F, was what might be termed "strong arm work." While the averages were still below their July tops, Atlas Tack was in this mark up phase. The ability of this issue to continue its advance and to hold its reactions at less than normal correction levels was indicative of a continuing strong sponsorship, especially when one considers the fact that the price continued to advance persistently during reactionary periods of the market.

---

6 See *Low Priced Stocks, When and How to Buy Them* by Owen Taylor

The First Caution Signal

The first cautionary signal came at the zone G. There, when the stock reacted from 28½ down to 25½, we had the first sign of a change in the technical structure. However, sponsorship was still apparent in the zone F, to G, and, in fact, it continued until around the columns J and K. Some distribution was going on in the zone G to K. Note, however, that the sponsors were buying the stock on minor reactions and distributing it at the upper levels, they were buying and selling on balance, meanwhile reducing the size of their long position established in the zone A, to D2. A new semi-catapult developed at 29, in column H. After the reaction at G, all stops should have been advanced to a point close below the low established on that sell-off. Subsequent to the semi-catapult at 29, one should have been on guard. Stops should have been advanced close beneath the market. Surely one should not have allowed such an issue to come back more than 2½ to 3 points from its last high. Positions established at 4, at 8½, at 9, at 11, at 18½, and at 20½, all would now have shown substantial profits and should have been closely guarded by stops. Notice, here, that the main trend line "LT," intercepted the work area in column I, when the stock backed and filled in the 30 level. That was the final warning. Stops should have been advanced to just below the price of 30, and, on subsequent strength, moved up close beneath the market. Compare the mark up trend pitch with the pitch of its predecessors. The final mark up trend line, "FM," clearly showed that the insiders had distributed a great part of their stock to the public and were standing aside. The public then held the bulk of the floating supply.

Boardroom Observations

The mark up in column F, when the stock advanced from 18 to 26, occurred on increased volume, and it was there that many boardroom habitués, customers men, and others were attracted to the performance of Atlas Tack. The churning in the zone between F, and H, represented distribution on balance by the insiders and some short selling on the part of the more experienced boardroom traders. The mark up in column I, occurred on terrific volume. There was another sign for boardroom traders. Great turnover in the number of shares of this stock, many transactions in this issue which had theretofore been extremely scarce, and rarely printed on the ticker tape as it unrolled from day to day, were indications to the more informed tape readers and boardroom observers that the end was close at hand in Atlas Tack. Many began to sell the stock short from column H to column J. This condition is always apparent on Point and Figure charts when many half-point changes are recorded.

The Shorts Began to Cover

In the zone K to L, some boardroom traders who shorted this issue began to take in their short lines, and the sell off in the stock met temporary support due to short covering. However, the less cautious ones stayed short, for they knew that even at $15 per share the common stock of the Atlas Tack Corporation was still high in price. After the temporary demand on the part of shorts who were covering around 15, was met, further supply carried the stock down to 10, and, in the zone L to M, this issue found a normal level consistent with its actual value and reasonable prospects.

Point and Figure Analysis

Notice that the zone H, to K, represented a large number of figure changes while little progress was made in the advance of Atlas Tack. This occurred during a period when the balance of the market had shown considerable strength. The opposite technical action occurred during the July break. That was the final signal for students of the Point and Figure Method to close out their positions. Increased volume with lessened progress, and sluggishness in the advance, were all definite signs that the sponsors had unloaded their stock on the uninformed public. It was time to get out of the issue, and, as a matter of fact, to look for the first opportunity where the price broke a previous support level at an inverse catapult or semi-catapult and there go short of this issue. The sell off in Atlas Tack from the actual high of 34¾ to 9½, was indeed dramatic. On Saturday, December 16, Atlas Tack opened at 33½, and soon sold down to 32¼. Trading in the issue was temporarily halted. The next sale recorded was 4800 shares at 25. That day, the stock closed at 21⅝, and a few days later declined to the low of 10. Thus, you see that no matter where your stop would have been in Atlas Tack, the positions established at the cata- pult point or at any of the semi-catapult points before the advance would have netted you $25 per share, a handsome margin of profit from the first position established at 4, the second at 8½, the third at 9¼ or the fourth at 11. Of course, there is a big difference between $34 per share near the high and $25 per share, the point at which the first block was sold after trading stopped. It is an indication of the danger involved using stop orders in a thin market stock. Nevertheless, it permitted the taking of mighty fine profits for those who took advantage of the signals as they were clearly developed by Point and Figure technic.

XIII

The Main Trend and Major Cycle Culminations

I n order to illustrate how the Point and Figure Method will aid you to judge the capital movement trend and the major cycle crucial turning points, we have added Figures 27 (see page 118), and 28 (see page 119), one-point charts of the New York Times Average from June 1929, to the now historical break which occurred in October of that year. Figure 29 (see page 121), is a three-point condensation chart of the same move and Figure 30 (see page 123), is a five-point condensation chart. The data used to prepare the three- and five-point charts was taken from the one-point moves as plotted on Figures 27 and 28.

Critical Culmination Points Easily Detected

The four illustrations, charts Figures 27, 28, 29, and 30, represent the top zone of the biggest bull market ever witnessed in the entire history of finance. That top represents an important and critical zone in which an ideal test of this Method may be demonstrated. We have stated that the Point and Figure Method provides the means for judging the major as well as minor culminations of price movement trends. We add to this statement that this is the only Method which will always aid you to recognize the turn of the major cycle when the market changes from bull trend to bear trend.

The One-Point Chart–The Basis for Analysis

Figures 27 and 28 (see pages 118 and 119), depict all of the one-point moves of the New York Times Index during the critical period from June 1929, to the break in October of that year. In those few weeks some of the issues on the big board fluctuated over a range of hundreds of points. The market from June, to September, offered exceptional opportunities for profit on the long side and the breaks of September and October duplicated those opportunities on the short side. Not alone did this Method clearly show the top and the reversal from bull to bear trend at that time, but it will continue to do so again and again as the price path leaves its tracings for posterity.

Interpreting an Intricate Major Culmination

The fifty stocks which comprise the index compiled by the *New York Times*, and which we use for the purpose of illustrating the reversal of the technical action in 1929, were a fair cross section of the market, when it was fluctuating around the higher zones during the period under consideration. Any of the popular averages could have been used for the same purpose, — either the Dow Jones Industrial group, the *New York Herald Tribune* or the Standard Statistics group of ninety stocks. Point and Figure Method technic may be applied to the movements of any market composite index. For best results, we suggest that you be sure the index you use is a true representation, a reasonable cross section of the market, that it is fairly accurate and compiled by a responsible organization.

The First Temporary Top

In the spring and early summer of 1929, several widely known organizations began suggesting the liquidation of long positions and the establishment of short positions in anticipation of a major trend reversal. The vertical chart formations of the action of some stocks during that time began to appear as though the end was near to hand. You will see from the following discussion that the Point and Figure Method would have prevented such conclusions on the part of those who understood its technic.

116

We ask you now to turn to charts Figure 27 (see page 118) and 28 (see page 119). In Figure 27, the zone A, to B, represents a trading area in the month of June which misled many vertical line technicians. We are sure that you will recognize it as a Point and Figure pattern with a **bullish** implication. The run up from column A, to the high at 248, in the middle of the zone was a sharp one, and a reasonable reaction should have been expected to correct so sharp an up move. Therefore, the declines which terminated at 242, are to be considered normal in view of the nature of the previous run up. It is true that the small air pocket which occurred beneath the work area around the figure 245, might have been considered a minor bearish implication, but only so if the reaction would have carried substantially lower, canceling more than 50 percent of the previous rally. In the area above column B, however, you will notice a few rallies and declines which began to show important bullish signals.

The bottom at 242, was tested, and the decline stopped at 243. Thereafter, the succeeding decline stopped at 244, and the future rally created a catapult at 247, and a major trend semi-catapult at 249. No student of the Point and Figure Method would have failed to recognize the bullish implications of market action at that time. No one would have sold out long positions or established short ones. The technical action was decidedly bullish and, in addition, the theory of "the count" applied to the congestion area between A, and B, implied substantially higher prices.[7]

Semi-Catapult Point – Unusually Bullish Pattern

The congestion area A, to B, with its semi-catapult point at 249, was an unusually bullish pattern. It implied substantially higher prices, and the run up B, to C, followed. This mark up B, to C, was a spectacular run-in of the shorts who had established their positions during the spring and early summer prior to the zone marked B. Those sharp advances are typical of major operations and in this case they proved to be the means

---

7 The count method is more fully described in *Advanced Theory and Practice of the Point and Figure Method*. (Note from the publisher: This book is out of print.)

FIGURE 27   New York Times Average One-Point Chart (1 of 2)

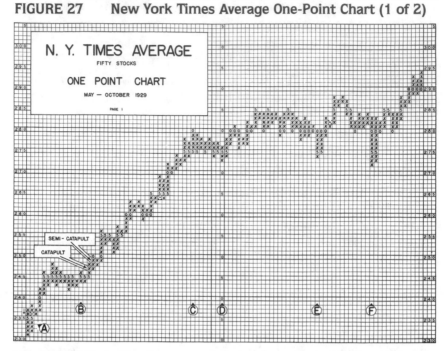

This chart and Figure 28 on the next page depict all of the one-point moves of the New York Times Index during the critical period from June 1929, to the break in October of that year. In those few weeks some of the issues on the big board fluctuated over a range of hundreds of points.

of obtaining front-page publicity for the market and an invitation which carried many of the public at large, head over heels into the biggest bull market ever witnessed.

Strength Carries Through Objective Level

The implications of the congestion area A, to B, suggested that the rally would run to at least 266, or higher, and it is at that zone that you would have had reason to begin to look for a possible top of the bull market.

In the zone 265, to 270, however, the market continued exceedingly strong and no danger sign occurred until the price area 275, to 280, began to develop. From the last starting point, 242, at B, to the tempo-

FIGURE 28   New York Times Average One-Point Chart (2 of 2)

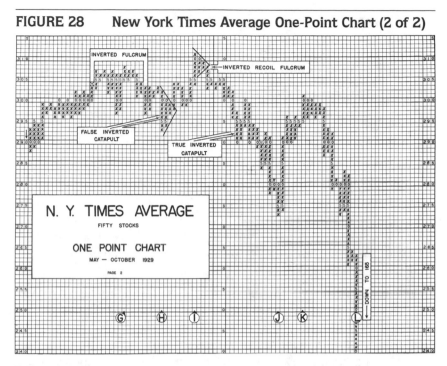

Notice the triangles between zones G and I and H and I, the inverted fulcrum at G, the false inverted catapult at full figure 296, and the inverted catapult point at 292 between columns I and J. These were all vital and important signals that clearly indicate the top of the bull market and its impending reversal.

rary top, 280, at C, we have had no correction of consequence. Examine the three- and five-point charts, Figures 29, and 30, and notice the sharp trend of the rally B, to C. Active short swing traders, basing their judgment on the one-point moves, would have liquidated positions around the 275 zone, sidestepping the market until either a correction was witnessed or until the semi-catapult point at 281 was registered. The rally A, to C, required either a congestion area of re-consolidation, or a reaction sufficient to correct so sharp an upswing. The reaction which came was of minor consequence, however, as is shown between columns C, and D. It was clearly indicated at this point from the bullish pattern and the solid formations which were witnessed between C, and D, that a further advance in prices was in prospect.

The Change Over of Technical Action

Observe carefully the zones between D, and E, between E, and F, the final mark up F, to G, the minor correction G, to H, and the false rally H, to I, with its inverted recoil fulcrum. Note the signs of distribution subsequent to the zone marked D. Observe that the highest squares between the work areas are massed solid with the oft repeating sharp declines followed by sharp rallies. These are always signs of the beginning of distribution and the weakening of the technical structure of the market. Stocks in this zone began to come out of the strong boxes, to pass from the hands of the insiders and long-term holders into the floating supply and to the inexperienced public who buy at the top of rallies and sell on the declines. Notice that the zone from D, to I, repeats again and again the elongated hollow areas beneath the work zones as the price path pattern progressed slightly higher and moved across our chart. Notice the absence of solid zones of consolidation. Observe that the move was struggling and meeting additional resistance as it worked higher.

Note carefully that patterns which have the form of the character "M," with the congestion work areas at the tops of the "M" loops, when repeated many times in rapid succession, are always to be considered of **bearish** implication. On the other hand, patterns which have the form of the character "W," with the congestion works areas at the bottoms of the "W" loops, when repeated many times in rapid succession, carry **bullish** implications.

The one-point moves as depicted on charts, Figures 27 and 28 (see pages 118 and 119), show many repetitions of the "M," pattern in the zone D, to I. This in accordance with the theorem set forth above, implies a weakening technical condition and constitutes an important cautionary signal.

On the three-point chart, Figure 29 (see page 121), the dips columns E, and F, indicate the beginning of a weakened technical position of the market, but the unusually sharp recoveries imply that the main top and reversal is to come from higher levels. In column I, you will note the reverse of these dips when the list rallied to 311, and quickly backed away. The action that quickly followed confirmed the last inverted catapult which had developed at 296.

FIGURE 29 New York Times Average Three-Point Chart

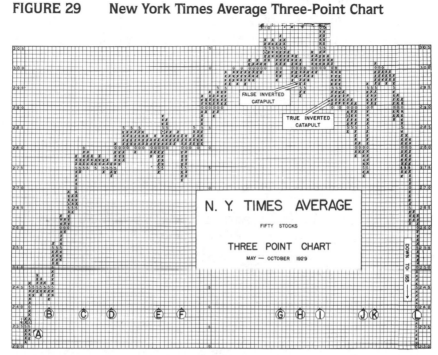

The dips columns E and F, indicate the beginning of a weakened technical position of the market, but the unusually sharp recoveries imply that the main top and reversal is to come from higher levels. In column I, notice the reverse of these dips when the list rallied to 311, and quickly backed away. The action that quickly followed confirmed the last inverted catapult which had developed at 296. The failure of the rally J, to K, to penetrate the main trend was final and definite confirmation that the bull market was finished and the bear trend started. Compare this chart to the one-point charts on pages 118 and 119.

Compare the one-, three-, and five-point charts at this point. Notice, on the five-point chart, Figure 30 (see page 123), that the final mark up trend line "FM," is soon intercepted by the price pattern just above the 300 mark.

The Top of the Move Clearly Indicated

The intersection of the price path pattern, by the final mark up trend line "FM," on the five-point chart was the all important danger signal, the final caution. That signal was confirmed by the nature of the patterns on the one-point chart, from zone D, to zone G. This, together with the failure of a mass zone of consolidation to develop between G, and I, were all to be considered as warnings of the impending reversal. The patterns recorded from column D, to I, constituted a change in the type of technical action and were caution signals for students of this Method to liquidate all long positions and stand aside until the previous rally, A, to H, was fully corrected. The correction could have been effected by either a congestion zone of consolidation or a reaction.

Indications of a Major Culmination

Notice carefully the peculiar and extremely nervous state of the market as was indicated on the one-point chart between zones G, and I. Observe the triangles on the one-point chart between zones G, and I. Observe the triangles at H, and I. Consider the fact that no consolidation of the final mark up appeared. Consider the inverted fulcrum at G, and the false inverted catapult at 296. Notice that the last push through at I, was accomplished without the previous formation of a firm solid base at 300. Also, consider the inverted catapult point at 292, between column I, and J. These were all vital and important signals for students of this Method; they clearly indicated the top of the bull market and its impending reversal.

Bear Trend Technical Action

Having reached the conclusions outlined in the foregoing paragraphs that the zones D, to I, represented a change in technical action, no student of this Method could have failed to recognize in the sell off from I, to J, and the rally J, to K, definite signs of an impending bear market and bear trend technical action. The top at I, is a typical inverted recoil fulcrum which you will recall always implies swift action. On the way down in the decline, full figure 303, represents the inverse catapult point. An additional inverse catapult is developed at 298. Certainly the failure of the decline to hold 299, and consolidate above that zone is an exceptional example of the imminence of a big break and an additional confirmation that buying power had been exhausted.

FIGURE 30   New York Times Average Five-Point Chart

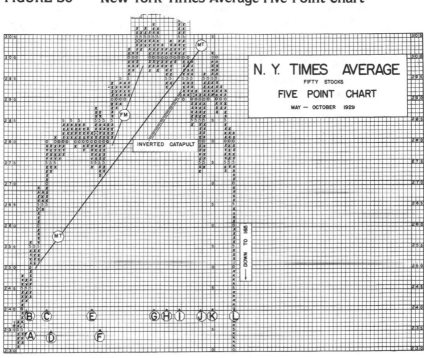

This chart clearly illustrates the turn of the major cycle when the market changed from bull trend to bear trend. Compare this five-point chart with the one- and three-point charts on pages 118, 119, and 121 and notice the warnings signals at key points on the charts.

You will remember, that a recoil fulcrum, whether upright or reverse, always connotes a sharp move impending. Therefore, either at 303, or at 298, you would have established short positions, especially so, if you were trading for the shorter swings based on conclusions and analysis of the one-point moves as depicted in Figures 27 and 28 (see pages 118 and 119).

The Investor or Long-Term Trader

The longer term trader, although he would have been out of the market, might have waited for further confirmation or an opportunity to analyze subsequent technical action before establishing his short position.

The decline I, to J, which started in September, and terminated temporarily in the beginning of October, was typical bear trend action. The recovery J, to K, was final and definite confirmation that the bull market was finished and the bear trend started. The congestion area which built up after the rally in column J, in the zone around 295 to 300, above the symbol "K" showed definite resistance and plentiful supply of stock for all buyers who wished to take it. The failure of the rally J, to K, to penetrate the main trend was a final confirmation of the bear trend even for the more cautious long-term traders who would have been out of the market during the decline I, to J. After the rally J, to K, with its inverse catapult at 289, inverse semi-catapults at 286, and 272, none could have doubted that the bear market was under way.

XIV

Technical Indications at a Turning Point

By observing the number of full-point or half-point changes recorded daily, either by individual issues or by a market index, and by studying the technical action throughout the day's trading and its relationship to immediately preceding market action, we are able to judge minor swing turning points.

The Change to an Up Trend

After a period of decline in a bull market, a turning point from **down trend** to **up trend** usually develops in the following manner:

1. The number of full-figure changes dries up (lessens) on the declines.

2. The number of full-figure changes increases on the rallies.

3. A test of the last established low point follows, which test must hold at a level above the last low or at the same point as the last low. The latter technical action is known as a double bottom, the former as a higher bottom.

4. After the test establishing a higher bottom or a double bottom, the succeeding rally develops sufficient strength to penetrate the preceding rally top.

(Students will note that the foregoing type of technical action exactly meets the requirements of the Point and Figure fulcrum formation.)

125

After a period of decline, it is customary, during periods of accumulation, for market activity to subside to such a degree that often many days may pass in succession wherein only 20 or 25 issues of the 100 most actively traded will show but one full-figure change daily. Students must remember that a limited number of full-figure changes after a decline is an indication of an impending turning point. In such a period, one should not feel that the market is inactive, or to use the colloquial expression, "doing nothing." It is at such times that important accumulation is being completed.

Changes in trend occur when the half-point half-hourly index hovers around a given level and builds up a congestion area from the few half-point changes which register each day. This is especially indicative of a changeover of trend when it occurs at or near one of the trend lines.

The Change to a Down Trend

After a period of advance in a bull market, a turning point from *up trend* to *down trend* usually develops in the following way:

1. The number of full-figure changes increases within a congestion area while the rest of the list rallies—buying power is temporarily exhausted as stocks pass into the hands of weak holders.

2. The number of full-figure changes increases on the successive declines.

3. A test of the last established high point follows, which test must fail at or lower than the last high point. The former technical action is known as a double top, the latter as a lower top.

4. After the test, the succeeding decline gathers momentum as it goes down and breaks the support point of the last previous decline

(Students will recognize this to be the type of technical action which meets the requirements of an inverted fulcrum.)

After an advance, it is customary, during periods of distribution, for activity to increase. In such periods, stocks fluctuate with increased numbers of full-figure changes but make little further progress or the rate of progress is greatly reduced as the number of fluctuations increase.

Conclusion

Success in every field of endeavor is but the result of assiduous effort towards a definite objective. In order to attain success, we must apply the principles which have aided others. In applying these principles to our own problems, we are, in effect, making the experiences of others our own.

Ofttimes the progress is slow and discouraging moments arise. When such obstacles do occur, the mettle of the individual is put to test. If he permits discouragements to impede his progress and concludes that he is incapable of accomplishment, he drops by the wayside and is overtaken and passed by those whose tenacity of purpose and determination to succeed is uninfluenced by temporary discouragement. To the successful these obstacles are merely additional incentives.

In the preceding chapters, we have endeavored to teach and to illustrate the basic principles of the Point and Figure Method of anticipating stock price movements. This Method has run the test of time and has not been found wanting.

Since a proper assimilation of the principles of this Method and their correct application to market action are the keystones to the mastery and acquisition of a knowledge of a stock market technic which cannot but pay handsome dividends, we urge you to keep the following guides before you at all times:

1. Apply yourself to a serious study of this Method. Ground yourself thoroughly in **all** of its principles and their application as set forth and illustrated in the text.

2. Apply the acquired knowledge to past as well as present market action. Test and retest your reasoning and conclusions. Money need not

be involved at first. Theoretical trades will be found interesting and instructive. They will give you the required familiarity with the proper application of the principles, and thus you will be instilled with that confidence so essential to success.

3. Having acquired a mastery of the principles of this Method, and a knowledge of their correct application, be sure to follow their implications. Have the courage of your convictions, and do not permit yourself to be influenced by outside opinions, rumors, or gossip.

The success achieved and the profits derived from your stock market transactions will be in proportion to:

- the enthusiasm with which you study the principles of this Method and their application,
- your understanding of the technical action of the stock market,
- the intelligent application of these principles to your own market operations.

Do not hesitate to consult the authors should you encounter difficulty.

Compendium
of Charts

▲▲▲▲▲▲

FIGURES 1 through 30

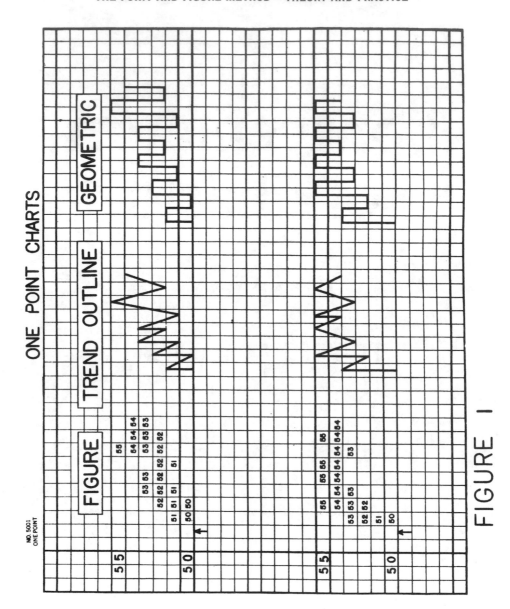

FIGURE I

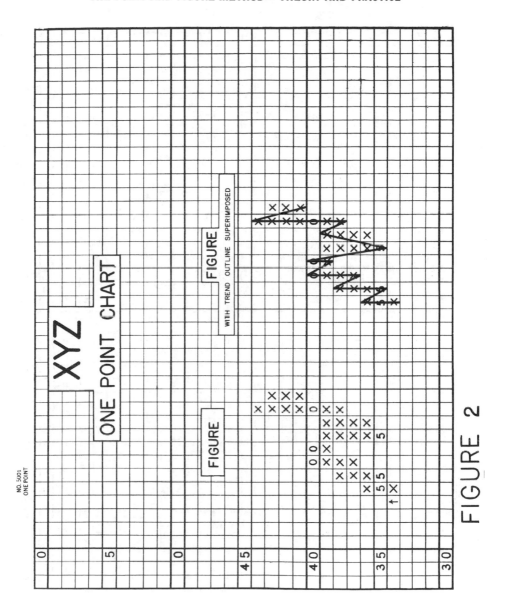

FIGURE 2

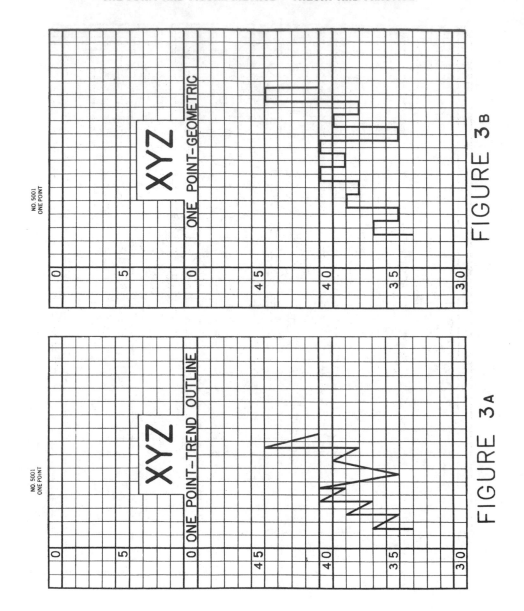

FIGURE 3ᴀ

FIGURE 3ʙ

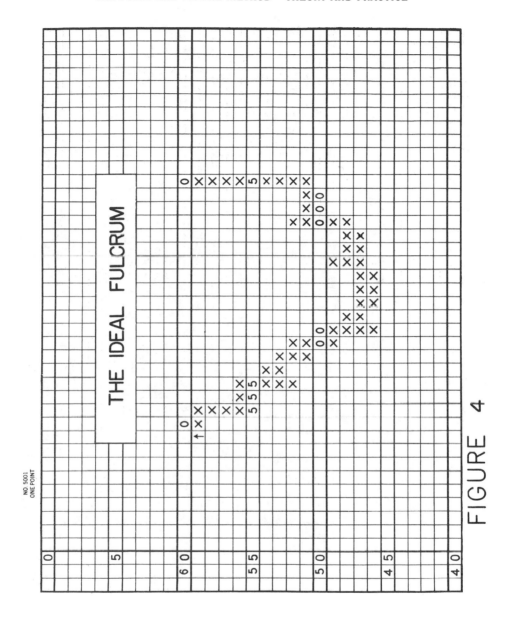

FIGURE 4

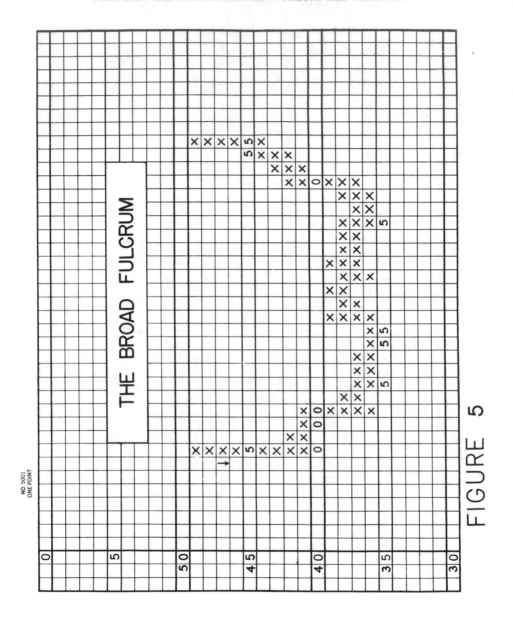

FIGURE 5

134

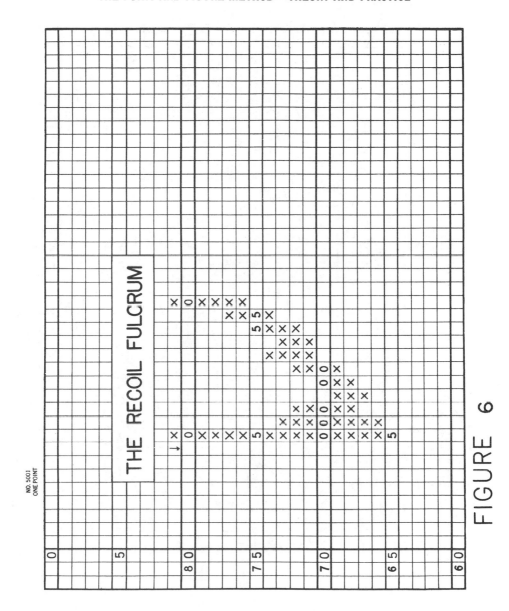

FIGURE 6

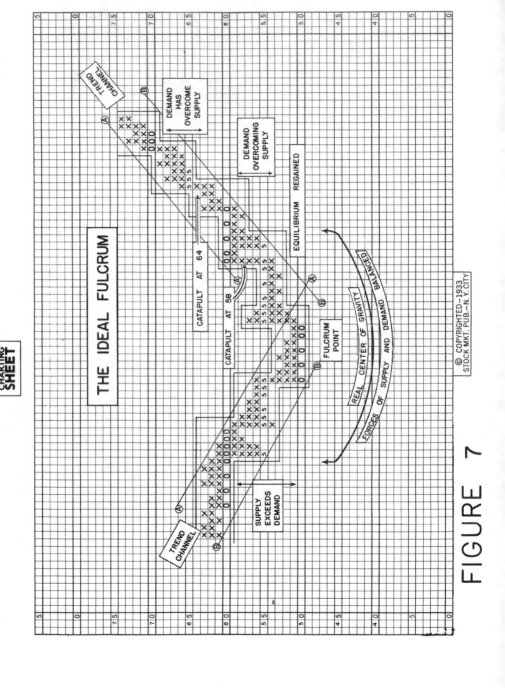

FIGURE 7

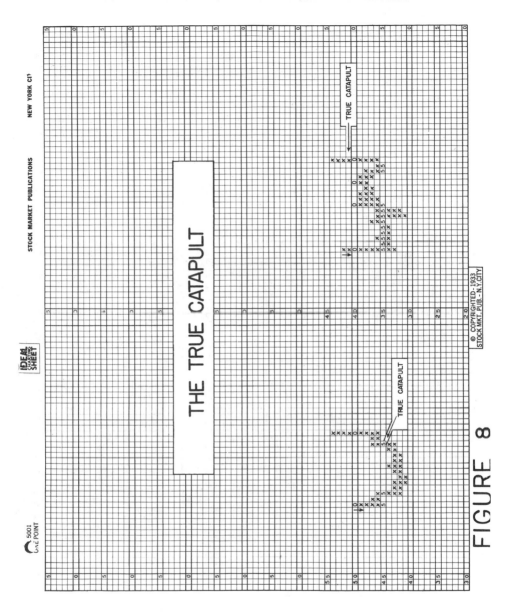

FIGURE 8

FIGURE 9

THE FALSE CATAPULT

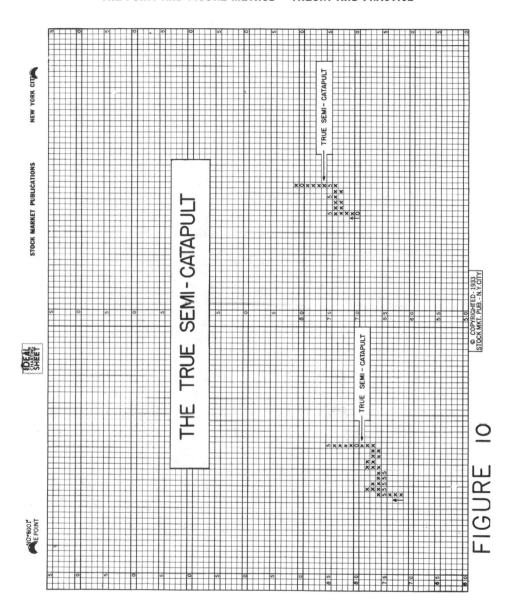

THE TRUE SEMI-CATAPULT

FIGURE 10

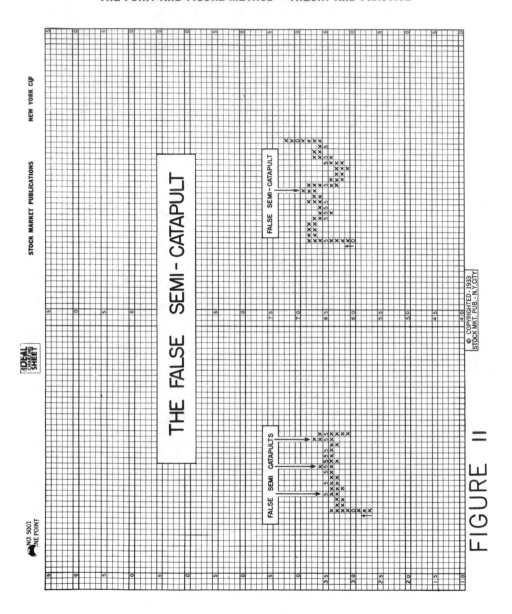

THE FALSE SEMI-CATAPULT

FIGURE II

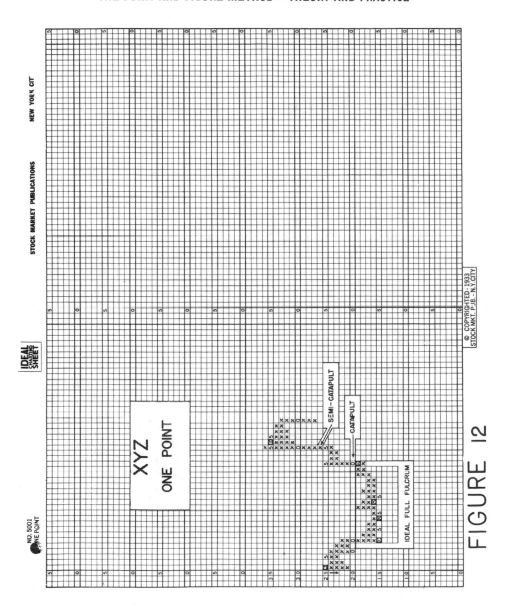

FIGURE 12

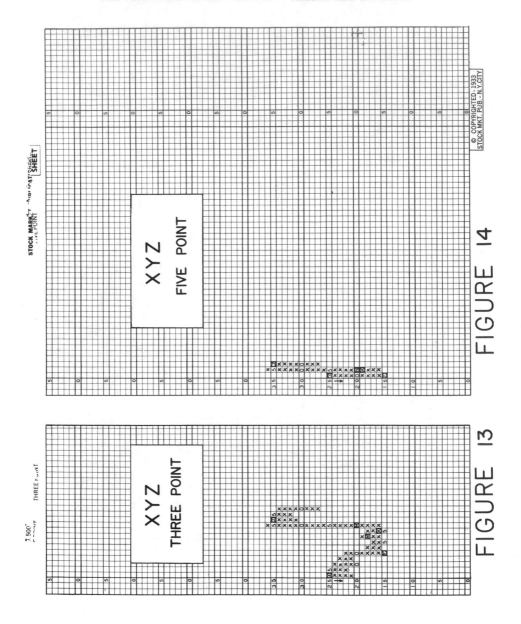

FIGURE 14

FIGURE 13

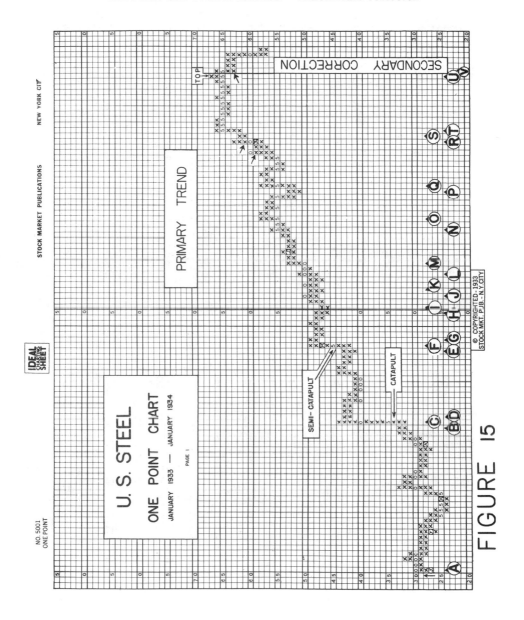

FIGURE 15

FIGURE 16

FIGURE 17

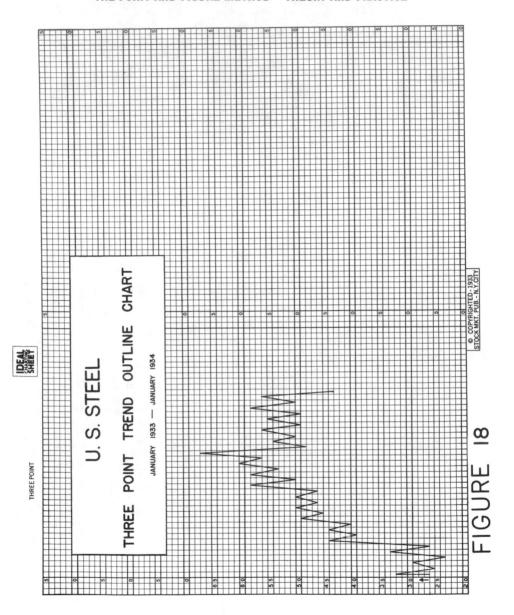

IDEAL CHARTING SHEET

THREE POINT

U. S. STEEL

THREE POINT TREND OUTLINE CHART

JANUARY 1933 — JANUARY 1934

© COPYRIGHTED - 1933
STOCK MKT. PUB. - N.Y. CITY

FIGURE 18

U. S. STEEL

THREE POINT CHART

JANUARY 1933 — JANUARY 1934

FIGURE 19

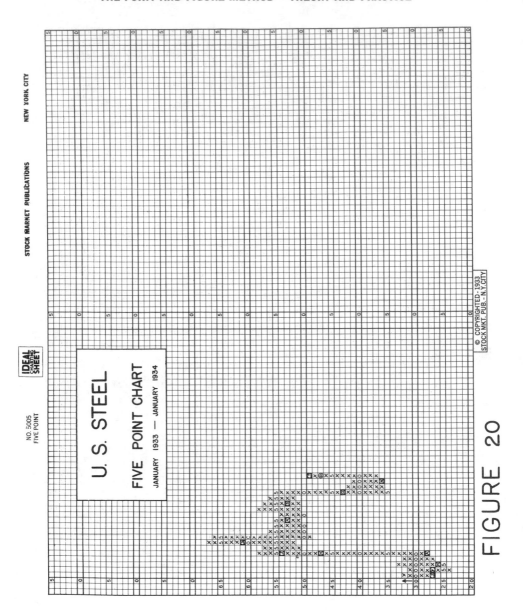

FIGURE 20

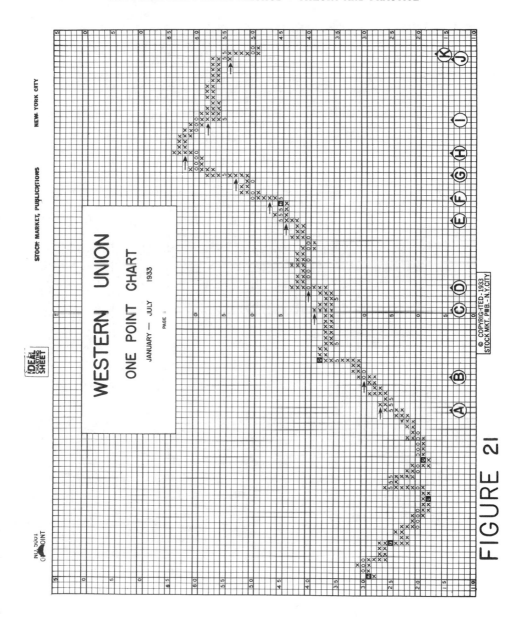

FIGURE 21

WESTERN UNION
ONE POINT CHART
JANUARY — JULY   1933
PAGE 2

FIGURE 22

FIGURE 23

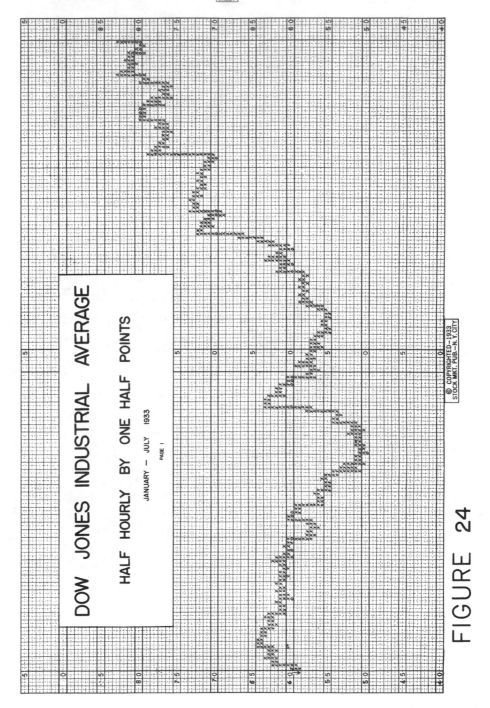

DOW JONES INDUSTRIAL AVERAGE

HALF HOURLY BY ONE HALF POINTS

JANUARY — JULY 1933

PAGE I

© COPYRIGHTED—1933
STOCK MKT. PUB.—N.Y. CITY

FIGURE 24

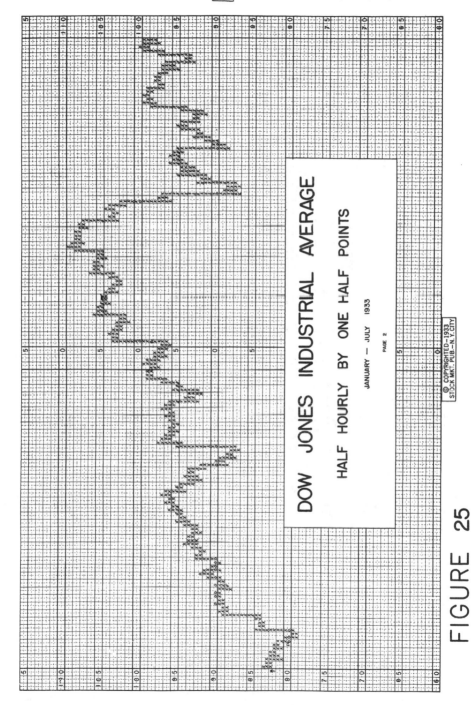

DOW JONES INDUSTRIAL AVERAGE

HALF HOURLY BY ONE HALF POINTS

JANUARY — JULY 1933

PAGE 2

FIGURE 25

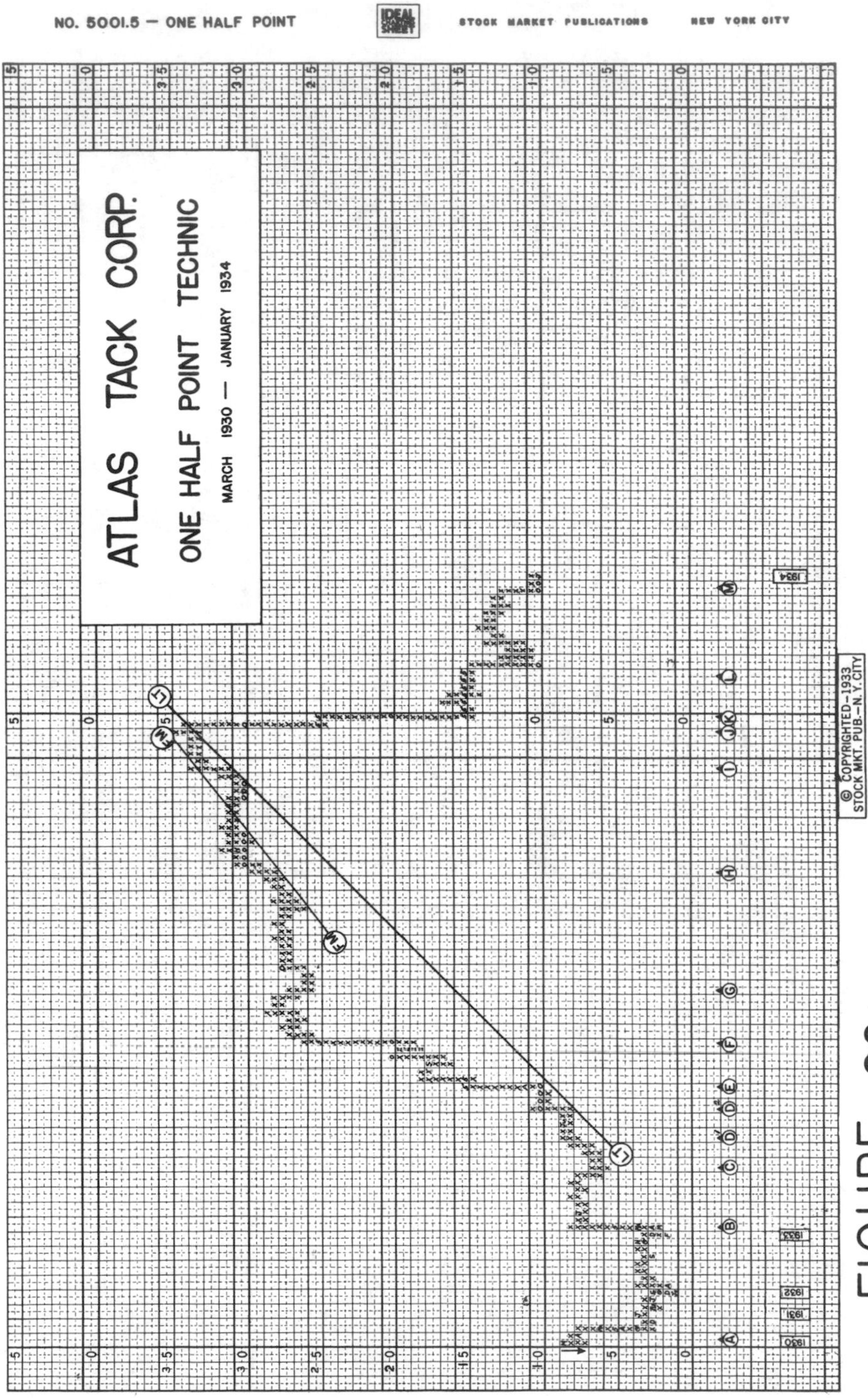
NO. 5001.5 — ONE HALF POINT
IDEAL CHARTING SHEET
STOCK MARKET PUBLICATIONS
NEW YORK CITY
ATLAS TACK CORP.
ONE HALF POINT TECHNIC
MARCH 1930 — JANUARY 1934
© COPYRIGHTED—1933
STOCK MKT. PUB.—N.Y. CITY

FIGURE 26

N. Y. TIMES AVERAGE
FIFTY STOCKS

ONE POINT CHART

MAY — OCTOBER 1929

PAGE 1

FIGURE 27

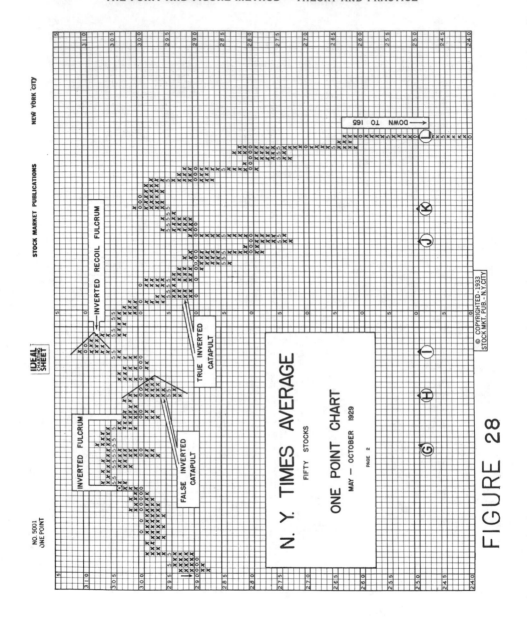

FIGURE 28

N. Y. TIMES AVERAGE
FIFTY STOCKS

ONE POINT CHART
MAY — OCTOBER 1929
PAGE 2

INVERTED RECOIL FULCRUM

INVERTED FULCRUM

TRUE INVERTED CATAPULT

FALSE INVERTED CATAPULT

DOWN TO 165

NEW YORK CITY

STOCK MARKET PUBLICATIONS

IDEAL CHARTING SHEET

NO. 5001
ONE POINT

© COPYRIGHTED - 1933
STOCK MKT. PUB. - N.Y. CITY

156

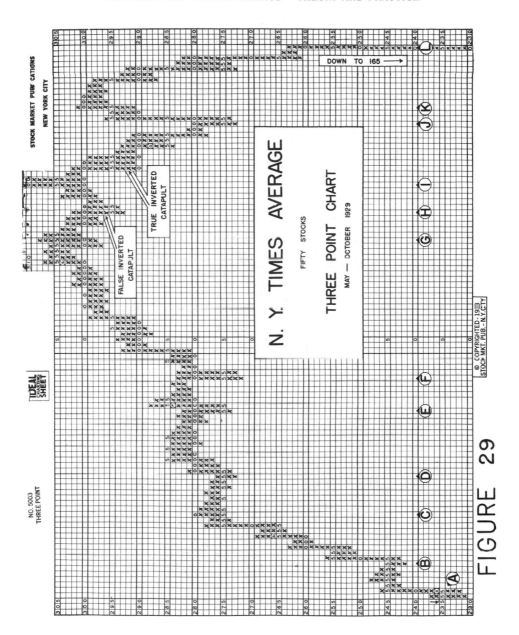

FIGURE 29

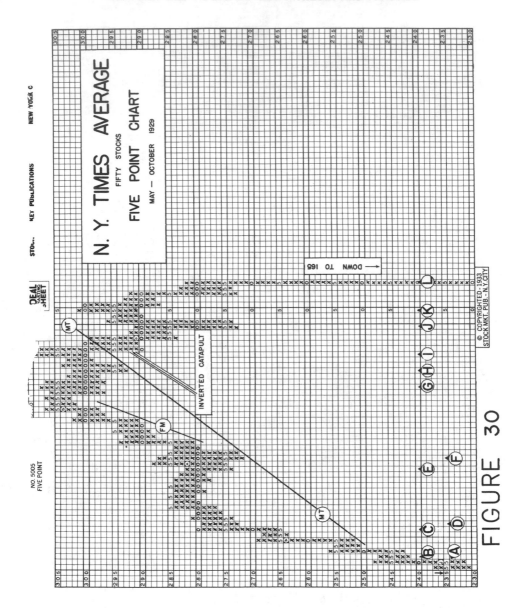

FIGURE 30

Trading
Resource
Guide

▲▲▲▲▲▲▲

TOOLS FOR SUCCESS
IN TRADING

Trading Resource Guide

Point and Figure Charting: Essential Applications for Forecasting and Tracking Market Prices
by Thomas J. Dorsey

Everyone loves Dorsey and his technical analysis classic. This brand new 2nd edition shows new and experienced investors alike how to bring charting into the Internet age. Discover cutting-edge new techniques to help you create, maintain and interpret your own Point & Figure charts.

$59.95. Item #BC108x12204

Charting Made Easy
by John J. Murphy

Renowned market technician John Murphy presents basic principles of chart reading in easy-to-understand terms. In the book he covers all types of chart analysis, "need to know" concepts such as trendlines, moving averages, reversal patterns, price gaps, price patterns and more. This book will also teach you how to use the industry's top tools to obtain a better understanding of what charts can do—and how they can help you grab your portion of today's trading profits.

$19.95. Item #BC108x11353

Introduction to Point & Figure and Candle Charting (DVD)
by Kenneth Tower, CMT

In a valuable cameo appearance, market legend Kenneth Tower comments on how you can combine point and figure charts with bar charts. Far from a dry presentation, Ken relates chart patterns to the real world of market emotions, addressing the What, Why, and How of price action.

$29.95. Item #BC108x4013411

Point and Figure (DVD)
by Bruce Kamich, CMT

If you've been using the 3-box method exclusively, you'll find "new" perspective that's actually a century old, yet useful for intraday analysis. Kamich was part of the legendary team that maintained point and figure charts by hand at prominent Wall Street firms for decades. Get the context you need from this seasoned pro!

$79.95. Item #BC108x4013414

Technical Analysis Simplified
by Clif Droke

Here's a concise, easy-reading manual for learning and implementing this invaluable investment tool. The author distills the most essential elements of technical analysis into a brief, easy-to-read volume. Droke's compact guide is a great starting place—and the perfect complement to any technical analysis software program.

$29.95. Item #BC108x11087

Trader's Guide to Technical Analysis
by C. Colburn Hardy

Achieving high-impact results can be made easier by implementing the most effective technical analysis tools throughout your trading day. In this easy-to-read classic, you will learn when to buy and sell stocks with the help of technical analysis—written for the average investor.

You will also learn to recognize trends and pinpoint entry and exit points, and how to improve trading results by combining technical and fundamental tools and techniques.

$37.50. Item #BC108x11563

Technical Analysis of Stock Trends, 8th edition
by Edwards and Magee

A universally acclaimed classic, updated with the latest data in market performance and trends, on which the foundation of technical analysis is built. Step-by-step coverage thoroughly explains and applies the current data. Stochastics, trendlines, stops, reversals, support/resistance, and tactical usage of each.

$99.95. Item #BC108x17379

▲ ▲ ▲ ▲ ▲ ▲

Many of these books along with hundreds of others are available at a discount from Traders' Library.
To place an order, or find out more, visit us at
www.traderslibrary.com
or call us at 1-800-272-2855 ext BC108

Free 2 Week Trial Offer for U.S. Residents From Investor's Business Daily:

INVESTOR'S BUSINESS DAILY will provide you with the facts, figures, and objective news analysis you need to succeed.

Investor's Business Daily is formatted for a quick and concise read to help you make informed and profitable decisions.

To take advantage of this free 2 week trial offer,
e-mail us at customerservice@traderslibrary.com
or visit our website at www.traderslibrary.com
where you find other free offers as well.

You can also reach us by calling 1-800-272-2855
or fax us at 410-964-0027.

This book, along with other books, is available at discounts that make it realistic to provide it as a gift to your customers, clients, and staff. For more information on these long lasting, cost effective premiums, please call us at (800) 272-2855 or you may email us at sales@traderslibrary.com.